THE GIRL WHO PLAYED HOCKEY

THE GIRL WHO PLAYED HOCKEY

A Story of Loss, Triumph and an Indomitable Heart

Chris Middlebrook

Editor: Jeff Z Klein
Cover Design and Layout: Kevin Bowen
Cover Photography: Shane Lines
Book Interior Design & Layout: James Arneson

ISBN: 979-8-218-13744-1

Published by:

Number 5 Publishing Company
Minneapolis, MN
USA

website: www.girlwhoplayedhockey.com
email: ccidbrook@aol.com

Printed in the United States

This book is dedicated to the Middlebrook Family:

To Delaney — a true warrior, the girl who played hockey, whose courage and determination were off the charts

To Cathy — every emotion from anguish to joy, we experienced together, every decision, we made together, every step, we took united

To Ian — who celebrated his sister's success while guarding her secret

To John and Phyllis — who loved their grandchildren, and shared the journey

To Alexander — our son who died at birth

And to Annalise — who wanted to live and fought so hard, but whose spirit was with her sister, Delaney, the entire time

If you look long enough into the abyss,
the abyss also looks into you.

~ *Friedrich Wilhelm Nietzsche*

CONTENTS

CONTENTS

Acknowledgments

Writing a book is not easy to do, and almost impossible to create by yourself. *The Girl Who Played Hockey* is no exception. It would not exist without the help and support I received from exceptional people. First and foremost is my editor and my friend, Jeff Z. Klein. His intellect, insight, recommendations and encouragement were essential to the finished product. Kevin Bowen conceived of and designed the extraordinarily powerful cover, together with Shane Lines, who did the front cover photography. Andrew Knutson read every chapter as it was written, and organized them so they could be presented to Jeff Klein. Jim Arneson created the interior design of the book. Steve Jecha was my guide to copyrighting the book. Greg Breining and David LaVaque, my writer friends, read the initial manuscript and told me that the story was powerful, moving and should be told. And finally there is Jeff Arundel, whose support and encouragement were essential not only to the writing of this book, but also my first book, *The Bandy Chronicles*, and who still confesses that I am a much better writer than he would have ever thought.

I. Looking Into the Abyss

Chapter I

I did not choose to look into the abyss. Instead God grabbed me by the back of the neck and forced me to look, longer and deeper than should ever happen. And the abyss looked back.

It is August 7, 1990, my 33rd birthday. I am at my office, meeting with a client, when Cathy calls. She is frantic. Her water has broken at 25 weeks, and she is on her way to the hospital. I leave immediately to meet her there. Twenty-five weeks is too early for our twin babies to be born. Their lives are in jeopardy.

August 11 is our sixth wedding anniversary. Cathy has been confined to her bed at Metropolitan Medical Center in downtown Minneapolis, with the hope that this will keep our twins inside her long enough to survive their birth. I sit by her side. We are tightly holding each other's hands as the doctor tells us that the birth of our children cannot be delayed any longer. At only 25 weeks, he says, nothing can be done to save them. They do not have the technology. Our children will die on the same day they are born. On the morning of August 12, 1990, their birth, and death, will take place.

There is no sleep that night, although any dreams could not be worse than our reality. Instead, for hours we listen in the dark to the *swoosh swoosh* of the heart monitor, the beat of three hearts within one body. Within hours only one will remain. And what words to say? There are none to convey or lessen our complete helplessness, the depths of our agony. Instead we simply lay side by side, holding onto each other until the nurses arrive, in the dark, to take Cathy to the delivery room.

I have called my parents that Sunday night to tell them our children, their grandchildren, will be born the next day. They arrive at the hospital at 6 a.m. They will not be allowed in the delivery room but they cannot stay at home, waiting to be informed of the inevitable ending. Instead, they intend to sit at the hospital, sharing the nightmare playing out in the daylight. Eventually, though, it becomes too much for them. They go back home, pull the curtains and sit in the dark, awaiting the final word.

In the delivery room the doctors and the nurses gather. There is also a Catholic priest. Cathy and I have asked him to be there to give the Last Rites to our children, He is young, perhaps even younger than Cathy and me. He is about to experience something they don't prepare one for in the seminary. It is now time for our children, our twin babies, to be born. Our baby boy comes first. His face is bright red, his features clenched. Even his tiny hands are clenched. He has died during his birth. Even so he is a beautifully formed little boy, strong looking, dark hair on his head. The nurses bring him to Cathy, so she can see her firstborn child, She lets out a wail of grief from the depths of her being, primal beyond measure. I ask the young priest to please perform the Last Rites for our baby boy. His response is to instead turn pale and then collapse into unconsciousness. A nurse revives him, and our dead boy, now wrapped in a blanket, is brought to him. He is able, barely, to perform his duty. I tell him that he can wait outside until our second child is born. We will then call him in to perform the Last Rites again.

Our second child is born. A girl, and she is alive, her heart visibly beating through her tiny chest. She too is perfectly formed and beautiful. She is brought to Cathy's arms and Cathy holds her baby girl for the first and last time. The doctor quietly says to me that Cathy is hemorrhaging internally. She will need emergency surgery or she will bleed to death. The priest is brought in again and performs Last Rites for our baby girl. He manages to maintain consciousness while doing so. Cathy then says a final goodbye to our daughter as she, still in the birthing bed, is wheeled to the surgery department. The nurses hand me our baby girl and get me a chair to sit in. They will give us as much time as we need. I sit in the chair, holding her on my lap. She and I will spend the rest of her short life like this, together. She is indeed perfectly formed. I can see, so clearly, the beautiful and amazing little girl and young lady she could have been. Her heartbeat is so strong. I can feel her telling me she wants to live. She is clearly a warrior. I am unable to tell her that this cannot be. After several hours the doctor returns to tell me that the surgery to stop Cathy's internal bleeding was successful. She will not die together with her children. I will go to see her when our daughter is gone. I will continue to hold our baby girl, to be with her, to let her know she is loved and not alone. For four hours her heart continues to beat. Each heartbeat, however, is like a star in her universe going dark. The final heartbeat comes, and all the light in the world that was her, goes out forever.

Chapter 2

Perhaps it is a ritual, formulated by experts on grief counseling and management to help those facing the sorrow and pain of the loss of their newborn children. Neither Cathy nor I are aware that the next morning a nurse will come to us in Cathy's hospital room, carrying our children, swaddled in tiny blankets, even tinier caps upon their heads, just as if they were alive. We each hold one of our children as the nurse asks what their names are. "Our boy is Alexander," we answer. "And our daughter is Annalise." "Those are beautiful names for your two beautiful children," the nurse responds. "I am so very sorry for your loss." She has brought a camera with her. "Would you like a picture of you and your babies? To help you always remember them?" A question we had not considered and were not prepared for. A photo of our dead children? Not a keepsake or a memento. We do not need a visual reminder, a photo of how awful life and death can be. We would prefer to remember our children as we choose to in our minds. That way we can have some control over how we remember. But, we say yes, and the nurse takes the photo. I have not looked at it since that day.

In the days and weeks that follow no one asks for any details on what exactly happened. How and why would they? We also have no desire or ability to describe and to relive.

Three months later, a great challenge arises. Cathy's younger sister has had a baby boy, and in early November the baptism takes place. We are the godparents. During the baptism and the party afterward I am certain that I am experiencing a major bout of PTSD. It is a struggle to keep from falling apart.

At one point during the party I am sitting with a next door neighbor, Herman. He and his wife Lydia, are both 80 years old. Herman tells me that he and Lydia tried for years to have children, but it never happened. In the 1930s and '40s their doctors were unable to understand or explain why they could not conceive. It has been the great sorrow of their life together. He tells me that God may have infinite wisdom, but such wisdom is beyond his ability to comprehend. It is also beyond mine.

With Christmas approaching, Cathy and I realize we are in need of some emotional support. We attend a group gathering at a local church, to help those who have lost children get through the holidays. Each speaker comes to the podium, prepared to tell us how they have learned to cope. Unfortunately, one after the other, each speaker breaks down, sobbing into the microphone. This is not helping Cathy and me learn to cope. We look at each other in horror, quietly agreeing that we are not benefiting from this gathering. Instead, we share a prayer, the same hope and plea. Please, God, give us another chance.

Chapter 3

He is about 2 years old, blond haired and blue eyed, happy in the unconditional way that only very young children can be, the unstained joy of being alive. I am struck by how much he looks like his mother. He is definitely Cathy's little boy. He grips my right hand tightly with the fingers of his left hand, reaching his arm above his head to do so. I am his father, but so much more at this moment than that. I am trust, I am love, I am his complete and unqualified protector. I am immersed in the total wonder of him. We are walking along an ocean beach, and yes, the sand is white, the cloudless sky completely blue, the water clear and sparkling. It is a perfect dream, more perfect than any I have ever experienced, and as I awake from this dream I also awake from a four-month nightmare, feeling both hope and certainty. Only days later, on the cusp of the Christmas holiday, we learn that Cathy is pregnant.

On August 3, 1991, Ian Young Middlebrook is born. And he is very much alive, kicking his tiny feet, his fists clenched, as he works his way to his first loud scream. The nurses clean him, wrap him in a tiny blanket, then place him in Cathy's arms. This time she holds her newborn son in complete euphoria. Welcome to the world, our baby boy. You cannot ever know how much you mean to us. Although Cathy and I did not technically know before his birth whether Ian would be a boy or girl, as we declined the offer to tell us during the many ultrasounds performed in Ian's nine months in Cathy's womb, I already knew. I had known since he and I walked together in my dream the previous December. I am certain that his eyes will be blue and at 2 years old he will have very blond hair, just like his mother, and that he will be happy and bring us great joy.

Chapter 4

Ian is so happy to be alive that it is nine months before he sleeps through the night. At first his crib is in our room so we can hear every movement, every burble, every exhalation. At six months he moves into his own room, colorful numbers on the wallpaper and stuffed animals on the shelves, together with the beginnings of a children's library. Even though Ian now sleeps across the hallway from our bedroom, I hear, throughout the night, even in my deepest sleep, every move and every sound he makes. One morning I hear that he has awoken. He is on his knees, hands holding the railings which keep him from falling out. He has a big smile on his face as I pick him up and lift him above my head, holding him in front of me. Ian then vomits directly into my smiling, wide-open mouth. I turn my head quickly to the right and so Ian vomits into my left ear. He then laughs, one of the first times I have heard him do so. I want to laugh too, but first I need to wash the vomit out of my mouth and ear. As he becomes a toddler and then a little boy Ian continues to exist with unbridled joy. After a heavy rain, when the alley is filled with thick, muddy water, he lies down and makes mud angels. He has a pair of green rain boots that have a frog head on the toe of each boot. He puts them on, and wearing nothing else comes out of his room and begins running in place , while making "shoosh-shoosh" sounds. We give him nicknames, of course. "Stinker Boy" which he thinks is so funny. "Buckster" which he doesn't like, as he informs me in no uncertain terms: "I'm not a buckster. I'm just a little kid."

And sometimes, Ian does things that he thinks are funny, but they instead put Cathy's and my hearts into our throats and emotionally bring us to our knees. At 2 Ian is playing in the backyard, in the turtle-shaped plastic sandbox. I have a ladder up against the house so

I can clean the leaves from the gutters. I go into the house to use the toilet and when I come out I see that Ian has climbed the ladder and is now sitting on the roof. At 3 Ian likes to play hide and seek, but thinks it is more fun when we don't realize he is doing so. He decides to play hide and seek by removing himself from his car seat in the one minute that Cathy and I are in the house after loading the car and strapping Ian in. The car is in the driveway. Cathy and I get in and I start the car. We then look into the back seat and see that Ian is no longer there. I stop the engine and get out to look for him. He is hiding behind the back of the car. Had we not noticed he was not in his car seat I would have backed over him. Nausea, both physical and emotional, overwhelms us. We put Ian back in his car seat and after a short time my shaking subsides so that I am able to drive. Decades later and this memory still dismantles me.

In June 1992 Ian is 10 months old. He is now sleeping through the night. Cathy and I are still perpetually exhausted but on a very warm night we are in the basement, watching television, and realize we have an opportunity to be intimate. We take advantage of this rare chance, but not before Cathy asks if we should take some precautions. We briefly discuss this but then agree that, with everything we have been through, it would be a miracle if something happened from this one interaction.

Chapter 5

Approximately nine months after that very warm June night, on March 30, 1993, our baby girl is born. Just as with Ian we decided that we did not want to know ahead of time what sex our baby would be. Even so, we are both quite certain that this child will be a girl. There is a predetermined pattern we have discerned. First a boy, then a girl. It has already been written. We have decided to name her Delaney to honor her Irish heritage but even more so because we love its sound and also because it is, at the time, a very uncommon name. When the Gaelic meaning is translated into English the name Delaney means "child of dark defiance," but we haven't researched this yet. Ultimately, we will learn that Delaney will become a child who defies the darkness. But that is years in the future.

Delaney arrives on an afternoon of ice and cold, somewhat unusual for Minneapolis at the end of March, 20 degrees colder than the average for that day. Unlike Ian, who comes into the world raising a fuss, newborn Delaney, although very alert, has a slight frown upon her face, as if sizing up Cathy and me along with her new surroundings. We have previously contemplated that because Ian so strongly resembles Cathy that Delaney will have the misfortune of looking like me. It is, however, impossible to form any opinions from looking at Delaney's face on that day. I bring 17-month-old Ian to the hospital so that he can see and even hold his sister. We sit him as far back as possible on a big cushioned chair and put her in his arms. His smile is genuine but also somewhat perplexed. Maybe this is like going to the petting zoo? Will Delaney be coming home with us or, just like the baby rabbits and goats, be staying behind? Cathy and I are not thinking these thoughts. We are instead basking in the balmy feeling of the four of us together for the first time as a family. She and I, our boy and our girl. Glorious. Sublime. The abyss that I looked into for too long is forgotten, for now at least, locked away in a heavily guarded and secured mental fortress, existing in the layer just below conscious thought.

Chapter 6

Delaney has come into the world with a heart murmur. Nothing to be concerned about, we are told, but she will be seen at the Children's Heart Clinic in Minneapolis on a yearly basis to make sure all is well.

Unlike Ian waiting nine months to sleep through the night, it takes Delaney only six months to accomplish this feat. And at six months she joins Ian at Community Child Care Center at the nearby Richfield Lutheran Church. Cathy or I drop Ian and Delaney off in the morning on our way to work, she as a lawyer for the State of Minnesota and me, also a lawyer, for Weinard, Webb & Middlebrook. One of us picks them up by 5 every afternoon. This will be our workday routine until they enter kindergarten, four years later for Ian and five for Delaney.

At CCCC the children are in separate areas, grouped by age. Ian is always in an older group than Delaney. He continues to be a good-humored, often hilarious, little boy whose merry charisma shines through in his words and actions, always plainly visible in his eyes and facial expressions. Delaney is much more reserved in expressing her happy emotions. Her first words, rather than presented in the singular, such as "mama" or "dada," arrive in the form of a complete sentence. In the summer of 1994 she is sitting in a stroller in the back yard. Several balloons are tied to the stroller. The balloons have her attention as they move about in the wind. Ian decides it would be good fun to pop one of the balloons. When he does so Delaney, speaking actual words for the first time, announces to Cathy and I, "That little boy, he's a stinker." Which he most certainly is.

At about 2 one of the little girls in Delaney's day care group becomes a biter. Over the course of a couple weeks she makes her way from child to child, even as the teachers attempt to put a stop to the biting. Eventually the biter decides it is Delaney's turn to get bit. This proves to be a big mistake by the biter. Delaney, we are told by the teachers, has been waiting for this and sees it coming. The biter grabs Delaney's arm, but Delaney pulls it away before the teeth can sink in. Delaney then grabs the biter's left arm and gives her a quick, but painful, bite in return. This is both the first and the last time Delaney bites anyone. It is also the last time the biter ever tries to bite anyone again at CCCC. A meeting is required by CCCC with Cathy and me to discuss what Delaney has done. We and she are not, however, chastised. Instead the three teachers gleefully tell us that they were waiting for the biter to make the mistake of trying to bite Delaney. They knew that Delaney would put an end to the biting, once and for all, and she did.

Ian and Delaney, even at such a young age, have decidedly different personalities. Ian is frogs and snails and puppy dog tails. Delaney is not sugar and spice. This is clear to us. She is instead a strong-willed little girl who at one point will motivate her grandfather to observe, "If you can keep up with her during her childhood and teenage years, you'll have one hell of an adult for a daughter." Although we had not previously considered the phenomenon, Cathy and I now both understand that much of what makes us who we are has been a part of us from the beginning of our existence in the womb. We will provide the nurture, as best we can, to support and guide the natures of our children, as we strive to do what all parents strive for, to give them every opportunity to be happy, successful and fulfilled. We know that we get only one opportunity to do so with Ian and Delaney, and that sometimes you don't get the opportunity at all.

II. The Ice Hockey Player

Chapter 7

In November 1997, 6-year-old Ian participates in ice hockey for the first time. In Minneapolis at that time there are four youth hockey organizations, each tied to a high school in a different section of the city and each presenting a varsity hockey team: Washburn, Southwest, South and Edison. At one time Minneapolis had 11 high schools playing varsity hockey; by 2010 there will be only one boy's high school team representing the entire city. (In 1997 there is also a Minneapolis girl's high school hockey team, the Minneapolis Novas, a two-year-old team consisting of players from all the city's high schools.)

Ian is starting in Washburn's Mini-Mite program, created for beginning hockey players. The players range in age from 5 to 9, and most are boys. Cathy and I have no aspirations for Ian to become a star player, earn a Division 1 scholarship or turn pro someday. The thought has not even entered our heads. We do know that we definitely do not want to step onto the slippery slope of Minnesota youth hockey, which dictates that you will not make the team if you don't skate winter, spring, summer and fall. You will be left behind as your friends who do make the full-year commitment make the A team and you do not. Your position and prestige within your age group will suffer. Your parents will not be able to bask in the glow of your skill and success, confident in the knowledge that their kid is among the special, the elite.

In 1997 there are many thousands of youth hockey players Ian's age registered with Minnesota Hockey, including a couple thousand who are girls. No doubt many of their parents also plan to avoid the slippery slope, but it is also likely that a vast majority of these parents secretly dream that their kid will emerge as special and ultimately elite. Regardless, at some point, before they know it, it will be too late, they and their kid will take one step too far onto the slope and will have joined thousands of others in full pursuit of hockey glory.

Washburn Mini-Mite ice times begin on November 15, a Saturday, early afternoon. For the remainder of the winter the ice times are on Saturday and Sunday only. They take place on the mini rink at Parade Ice Gardens, in the Kenwood neighborhood, close to the Walker Art Center and Loring Park, a little more than a mile from downtown Minneapolis. Parade also has two full-size ice arenas that I remember well from high school when I played hockey for Washburn High. Ian is thrilled as we help him put on his equipment, shin guards, elbow and shoulder pads, breezers, his helmet, gloves and finally his skates. We then hand him his hockey stick. He has the same look on his face that he had two years before when under the tree on Christmas morning he discovers that Santa has left for him a plastic sword, shield and helmet, just like the ones the soldiers in the Roman legions carried.

Ian can already skate, as he and Delaney have had lessons at Richfield Ice Arena and I have taken him to Pearl park to skate on the natural ice in the winter. He and Delaney have also skated on the frozen slough, just off the Kickapoo River, in Cathy's hometown of Soldiers Grove, Wisconsin, wearing plastic skates that we bought for $10 each. Even so, he is maybe only two levels above a beginning skater. He steps onto the ice with 30 other kids from the Washburn area and begins to skate around the rink. There are five dads on the ice, running the practice. Other hockey communities may have non-parent coaches, even paid coaches, but in the Washburn youth program at the time, from Mini-Mites to Bantams, every coach, head or assistant, is a volunteer and a player's dad. Every team manager is a player's mom.

Cathy and I have brought 4-year-old Delaney with us to watch Ian's first hockey ice time. I hold her in my arms so she can see through the glass. She watches for 10 minutes, then turns her face to mine and does not ask but instead announces, "I want to play hockey."

"OK," I respond as I remember her swimming to the bottom of the eight-foot-deep end of the pool to retrieve a diving stick when she was only 3. "But if you are going to play hockey I want you to promise me that you will never cry or be a baby on the ice, always try your hardest, and most important that you will never, ever, be a quitter." Delaney responds to me with her high-pitched 4-year-old's voice, her face serious and determined, "I promise, Dad, that I will never be a quitter." That afternoon Cathy and I take her to the hockey store to buy her gear, including actual hockey skates.

The practice is over and the coach who has been in charge comes over to speak with me while Cathy helps Ian take off his equipment. His name is Bill Butler and he is also a former Washburn hockey player, but six years younger than me. "I know who you are—I used to watch you play for Washburn when I was a kid," Bill says to me. "Don't think your kid is going to skate in this group if you're not going to be one of the coaches. Don't show up tomorrow unless you bring your skates and stick." He concludes with "See you tomorrow."

Yes, I played hockey for Washburn and then college hockey for Gustavus Adolphus. I have also played bandy, a sport closely related to hockey, for many years in the U.S., and I have been player and coach of the U.S. national team. I also played bandy professionally for two years in Sweden, and I've skated and coached on bandy rinks all over the Nordic countries, Russia and elsewhere in the northern world. But I did not have a burning desire to coach my own kids in youth hockey.

Even so, the next day I show up with my stick and skates—the start of a nine-year journey coaching Ian and Delaney in Washburn youth hockey.

Chapter 8

With Mini-Mite hockey comes a new set of friends and a new social network. This will be our reality from October through March for the next eight years. Youth hockey in Minnesota exerts a powerful and mostly positive socially gravitational force. The 5- and 6-year-old boys Ian will grow up with on hockey rinks as well as on soccer fields, at lakes and swimming pools, and on PlayStations and Nintendos, will become lifelong friends. Cathy and I and the other parents become part of a social network that revolves around our kids and their sports, especially hockey. In the years to come, from October through March, we are together at the hockey rinks, and afterward at the pizza parlors or at Adrian's Bar for hamburgers and 3.2 beer, and eventually at out-of-town tournaments, sitting poolside at a Holiday Inn.

Our collective time as hockey parents is both fulfilling and precious, though none of us are thinking about this at the time. It is only when the years have passed, and our kids have gone their separate ways in hockey and in life, that we realize how fantastic it all was and how fortunate we were to have been a part of it.

There are only a few girls besides Delaney skating with the Washburn Mini-Mites in 1997-98. There is only one who is memorable. Her name is Nicole. She has just turned 5 years old in November. She is tiny and quiet, but she is as focused and determined as Delaney. Nicole and Delaney are drawn to each other, not just because they are two hockey girls in a sea of little boys. They become friends and will skate on the same Washburn team for the next four years. They will never become true rivals, but ultimately they will come into indirect competition among the girls in their age group as they climb the hockey ladder. In the future they will strive not just to make their own youth association teams, but also to play on the best AAA teams which compete in high-level tournaments from spring through fall. The hockey goals of these players, shared by and often more important to their parents, evolve into playing on a good high school team, with the hope of making the state tournament, all while standing out as a top-level player. The ultimate prize, however, lies beyond the high school team—playing college hockey at the D1 level.

Cathy and I have no awareness of any of this potential future during the Mini-Mite winter of 1997-98. We are just happy that Ian likes hockey and has made new friends. We are also happy that our swim-to-the-bottom-of-the-eight-foot-deep-pool Delaney, the girl we have nicknamed Powerhouse, now has skating and hockey as an outlet for her energy and determination during the long winter months.

Chapter 9

The next step up the Washburn youth hockey ladder from Mini-Mites is Mite C. I am now the head coach. My youngest players on the 1998-99 team are Delaney at 5 years old and Nicole at 6. Ian and his growing cadre of hockey boys make up the majority of the remaining skaters. Mite C still primarily consists of practices, some at the mini-rink at Parade Ice Gardens, but now also on the full rink. On the big ice the players skate around like puppies swimming in an Olympic-size pool. Their parents attend each practice, not because they are monitoring the development of their children or the practice plans of the coaching staff, but because they are necessary for driving their kids to and from the rink and to lacing their skates tightly. Most meaningfully, the parents get to watch their kids skate and play hockey for the pure fun and joy of it.

There is no pressure, no stress that comes with this hockey. There are even no set goalies, as every kid who is willing takes a turn between the pipes. The highlight of the winter are the very first games against the Mite C team from Minneapolis Southwest. The coaches are the referees, actually the monitors and cheerleaders on the ice. The puck is dropped and wherever it goes it is followed by every skater on the ice. Any goals that are scored are accidental, yet they are celebrated as monumental occurrences.

The Washburn players improve, particularly in their skating, as the practices focus on this skill. It is important, however, to mix the skating with the fun. Skate as fast as you can to the blue line then drop to the ice and see how far you slide. Obstacle courses through prearranged cones. A mini game at the end of each practice between the players and the coaches. The players win every time.

"Wouldn't it be fun to have a couple real games?" the parents ask. "With referees and against teams other than Southwest? Look at how the kids have improved."

"Yes," I agree, "it would be." In March 1999 there is a Mite C tournament at the new indoor rink in Siren, Wisconsin, 110 miles from Minneapolis. Cathy and I know the area well; we have land on a lake nearby that we are building a cabin on. Siren even has a brand-new hotel with an indoor heated pool. I present this idea to the parents, and they vote unanimously that the Washburn Mite C team should enter the tournament. We submit our registration and book our rooms.

I have assumed that Wisconsin Mite C is similar to Minnesota and Minneapolis Mite C—relatively new players, primarily ages 5 to 7, like the Washburn team. I am mistaken. Wisconsin categorizes their Mite levels by the size of the city or town the hockey program draws from. Siren has a population of only 800, although they draw players from even smaller surrounding towns. Even though they have multiple skaters up to 9 years old, under Wisconsin hockey regulations they are a Mite C team, the Burnett County Blizzard. The other teams in the tournament are all also from Wisconsin. The Washburn Mite C team is the youngest team in the tournament. Delaney and Nicole are among the smallest players.

Three games are played: 12-1 and 6-1 losses, but the final game a 1-1 tie as Ian scores his first goal ever. The kids could care less about the results. They spend most of their free time in the hotel swimming pool. The parents are reluctant to be in the pool with the kids as they become climbing poles or tossing-the-kids-into-the-air machines. John Behm takes one for the parent team, spending several hours in the pool as the fun dad. As the weekend ends it is clear that both kids and parents alike have had a wonderful time.

I learn a couple weeks later that Minnesota Hockey prohibits Mite teams from playing games or tournaments in other states without first obtaining permission. No permission was requested by the Washburn Mite C team, and as the head coach and the man in charge of the weekend I am to blame. I receive a sanction from Minnesota Hockey and am put on probation.

Sanction or not, the weekend was still worth it.

Chapter 10

Delaney's Mite career in the Washburn Youth Hockey Program lasts five years: Mite C as a 5- and 6-year-old, Mite B as a 7-year-old and finally, in the 2001–02 season, Mite A as an 8-year-old third-grader. Nicole and Delaney are teammates for each of these five years, and I am their head coach.

After the initial Mite C season of 1998–99, Ian begins skating at a level above Delaney. I am no longer his coach. The Mite B season of 2000–01 arrives for Delaney and Nicole, and they are joined on the team by a third girl, Ali. Unlike the power youth programs (Edina, Roseville, White Bear Lake, Eden Prairie, etc.), Washburn and Minneapolis do not yet have Mite or Squirt-age teams for girls. If the girls want to play, they play on the boys' teams.

Measuring Washburn youth hockey against the other programs in the metro area, the best Washburn teams are at best a degree above the middle. The majority of the Washburn teams are a degree or two below. This includes the Mite teams that I coach and that Delaney and Nicole play on. We play in District One, which covers Minneapolis and St. Paul, and the suburb of Irondale. The games in District One hockey are, in effect, scrimmages. They are refereed by the coaches, who are allowed to instruct and encourage their players on the ice. In one of these Mite C games, on January 6, 2000, against St. Paul Como, 6-year-old Delaney scores her first goal, skating the puck in from the right point and shooting low along the ice, where the puck somehow goes under the goalie and into the back of the Como net. Yes, I take the puck from the net and put it into my coat pocket.

Each of the District One hockey associations faces the same hurdles as Washburn: not only a lack of numbers and for many a lack of financial resources, but also an overall rejection of making hockey a year-round sport for their young children. Perhaps this is also attributable to parents' realization that their kids will be unable to compete at higher levels against the players from the power youth programs. Consequently, District One games are competitive, and continue to be so through Squirt and Pee Wee. But care must be taken when deciding which tournaments the teams are scheduled for so that they don't play in competitions filled with first- and second-tier power hockey associations.

Sometimes, however, these games do take place, usually in the first round of a tournament where the host team schedules so that they play Washburn first. One game, however, does stand out—a Mite B tournament contest against host Woodbury. The final shots on goal were 34 for Woodbury, and 1 for Washburn. The final score: Washburn 1, Woodbury 0. That result is an exception, as success for the Mite teams I coach is not measured by winning (although winning still feels real good), but by the effort and intensity the players put out, both in games and in practices, the improvements in their hockey abilities from season's beginning to its conclusion and, most importantly, the positive experience, the fun, that they've had playing hockey and being a part of the team. Just as important is how the players' parents feel about the season.

One thing becomes clear: Delaney and Nicole play with as much intensity and desire as the boys on the team, if not more. They, together with Ian, are the first to sign up for a skating clinic I offer to run, uncompensated, for Washburn youth hockey in the spring of 2002. I rent ice at both Parade and at Highland Arena in St. Paul. The clinic fills up completely. It is a success, so much so that I organize another skating clinic in the fall. I will continue to run spring and fall skating clinics for Washburn through the fall of 2004. It is during one of the spring ice times at Highland Arena that Delaney applies the lesson that I have taught her and Ian: Don't ever let anyone bully you—put a stop to it immediately.

Actually, this was not a lesson I ever had to teach Delaney—it was already a part of her nature. In the dressing room at Highland, before the ice time begins, one of the boys, Jack, is teasing Delaney without mercy. With her skates on she walks over and stands in front of Jack. He laughs at her with a "What are you going to do?" expression. Delaney then grabs Jack by the forehead and smacks the back of his head into the concrete wall behind him. As Jack begins to howl I confront Delaney. She tells me Jack deserved it—he shouldn't have been so mean, and she is certain he won't be mean to her again. (She will be proved correct.) Even so, I tell her she can't go on the ice until she apologizes to the now sobbing Jack. She repeatedly refuses to do so until, just before the gate opens to go on the ice, she says, tears of rage coming from her eyes, "I'm sorry, Jack." But she is not sorry.

Chapter II

Even with the introduction of skating clinics, the spring, summer and fall do not revolve around hockey for the majority of Washburn Mite skaters, boys or girls. Instead they play soccer, baseball, softball. Ian and Delaney play soccer in a spring program called Fuller soccer. There are no practices, just six-on-six games. Everyone gets a T-shirt jersey. The coaches are all parents. I am one of the coaches. The Fuller philosophy is everyone plays, everyone has fun, no one is better than anyone else. We even go to Dairy Queen afterward.

In the fall Delaney also plays soccer, in a Minneapolis Park Board league at Pearl Park. Almost all the kids attend the neighborhood grade school, Hale. This is also a league that emphasizes participation over competition. The coaches are again all parents, including parents who never competed in sports other than kickball games back when they were in grade school. If soccer is to be fun nobody should try too hard. This mentality—playing soccer just for fun, nobody is better than anyone else—does not fit with Delaney's personality, which, Cathy and I are recognizing, comes from me. Recreation, not competition? Nobody is better than anyone else?

I am the coach of Delaney's team. Delaney and five other girls are on my team. None of the other girls have played soccer or any other competitive sport. But they are good athletes and very good students. I tell them that soccer, like doing well in school, is more fun if they put all their effort into it, just as they do with school. They respond with enthusiasm. The team wins every game by up to 10 goals. The girls are thrilled, but the parent coaches of the other teams are not. They are in particular not thrilled with me. I won't be coaching Pearl Soccer again. But just as significantly, Delaney has decided that she is done, forever, with just-for-fun, nobody-is-better-than-anyone-else sports. For her, sports are no longer simply recreation. They now have a purpose—to improve, to excel, to win.

Chapter 12

The winter of 2002-03 will be Delaney's sixth year of Washburn youth hockey. She is now a 9-year-old fourth grader at Hale School. Mite hockey is done. She is now at the Squirt level. This means playing in the District 1 league and in-town and out-of-town tournaments, plus scrimmage games against other teams in the Minneapolis/St. Paul metro area; Real referees and not parent coaches blowing the whistle; orange, blue and white uniforms with a big blue "W" on the front—could it get any more awesome? Yes! The players even have their last names on the back of their jerseys.

Washburn does not have enough girl skaters to present a U10 team. The girls instead must skate with the boys on the Squirt teams. This includes Delaney and Nicole. They are ready. For two weeks each summer since 2000 they have skated at the Top Dog Hockey Camp at Augsburg Ice Arena in Minneapolis, where the other skaters are almost all boys, including Ian. They and Ian also share in a weekly ritual of going to open skating at Parade Ice Gardens, one night each week, in the spring and fall. I am also on the ice, skating, as we play follow-the-leader and tag games, hold one- and two-lap races and conclude the evening with a five-lap skate. Nicole's mom, Gayle, joins us on the ice. Father Jeff is up in the stands. "Might as Well Be Walking on the Sun" by Smashmouth plays loudly on the arena sound system, and for years to come this song will become a memory trigger of spring and fall evenings open skating at Parade.

Washburn will have three Squirt teams in 2002-03. The Squirt A team, coached by George Perpich, is made up entirely of boys in the fifth grade. Ian skates with this team. Twenty skaters and two goalies remain. They are split into two Squirt B teams, the Orange and the Blue. I coach the Blue, where Delaney and Nicole are again joined by

Ali, and there will also be a fourth girl on the team, Jill, who has come over from the Minneapolis South youth program in a consolidation with Washburn youth hockey. The other Squirt B team, the Orange team, also has 10 skaters, all boys. It definitely comes as a shock to the boys on the Orange team, and their parents, when in November 2002, in a game to kick off Washburn Hockey Day, the Squirt team with four girls beats them, 4-2.

When the rematch occurs in February 2003 the stands at Parade Ice Garden are full, not just with the parents of the players from both teams, but also many others from the Washburn youth hockey community. Although Blue has only four girls on the roster, the game is seen as a boys-vs.-girls contest. The parents of the all-boy Orange team are verbal and loud during the warmups and throughout the game. The Orange coach and I make a bet before the game. We know that the players from both teams will be competing to make the Squirt A team the next season. Our agreement is that the coach of the winning team will coach the Squirt A's next season.

The game ends in a 4-3 victory for Squirt B Blue and the four girls on the team. The players and their parents are jubilant—it's the highlight of their hockey season. The triumph also confirms that I will be head coach of the Squirt A team the next season.

When the Squirt B Blue season concludes a couple of weeks later, Cathy and I discuss Delaney's abilities as a hockey player. She's a good skater, but unremarkable in comparison to her teammates and opponents. There is nothing about her hockey skills that stand out, other than her fierce determination and passion for the game. She loves to play hockey, and her being able to play is what matters to Cathy and me.

III. A Very Difficult Decision

Chapter 13

In the fall of 2003 Delaney's heart murmur, present since her birth, is recognized as something much more significant. Her doctor at the Children's Heart Clinic refers her to Dr. Michael Ackerman, a pediatric heart specialist at the Mayo Clinic.

Cathy and I drive her down to the Mayo, leaving our house at 5:30 on a Tuesday morning. There she undergoes multiple exams and tests, including a stress test in which she runs a treadmill at gradually increasing speed and incline while hooked up to a heart monitor. Very frightened, she is sobbing the entire time, tears cascading down her face, mixing with her sweat, before they fall onto the treadmill. The testing is not completed until mid-afternoon, and it is only then that we first meet Dr. Ackerman.

> *Miss Delaney Middlebrook is a most delightful asymptomatic 10-year-old white female. She has been seen at the Children's Heart Clinic for the past five years ... They have suggested that she come down for further evaluation.*

—Mayo Clinic records, Dr. Michael Ackerman notes, September 23, 2003

Dr. Ackerman's diagnosis is long QT syndrome, also known as "sudden death syndrome."

"Sudden death syndrome?" Cathy and I scream in unison, silently, but we can hear each other. "Sudden death syndrome?" This must be a joke or a mistake. It is the most unfair thing we have ever heard. Two of our children have already died and now we are being told that our determined, strong and athletic 10-year-old little girl, our Powerhouse, has sudden death syndrome?

Delaney sits wedged between Cathy and me as Dr. Ackerman proceeds to inform us on what long QT syndrome is. Delaney

THE GIRL WHO PLAYED HOCKEY

continues to sob, her entire body quaking, gasping for air as if all the oxygen has left the room. Dr. Ackerman explains that long QT is a heart condition, first described in medical journals in 1957. Long QT syndrome is relatively rare, affecting about 1 in every 7,000 Americans, more often females. For persons with long QT, issues occur when the heart is beating at a high rate, which can be caused by exercise or physical or emotional stress. A higher heart rate can cause the heart to beat irregularly, which can then lead to dizziness, fainting, even heart stoppage and death. These are termed "episodes." The long QT diagnosis usually occurs because someone has had an episode and an EKG then confirms the condition. (The term long QT comes from a longer-than-normal interval between the "Q" and "T" pulses in a heartbeat, a delay that is visible in an EKG.) An EKG, of course, is not possible if the first episode causes sudden death.

Through testing Dr. Ackerman determines that Delaney's long QT is genetic. She was born with her condition, known as "congenital long QT syndrome." The strongest predictor of whether someone with long QT will develop an abnormal heart rhythm is if they have had previous episodes; if they have had no previous episodes it is impossible to predict if they ever will. Most persons with congenital long QT never have a symptom, and never have an episode.

> *Again, her own presentation is completely asymptomatic. She has never had any symptoms attributable to long QT syndrome.*
>
> *She is very active in sports, including hockey and soccer.*
>
> *Clinically there is no doubt she has long QT syndrome.*
>
> *With this degree of QT prolongation, I would recommend beta blocker therapy ... even though she has been asymptomatic.*
>
> *To be sure, 40% of individuals with long QT syndrome can be lifelong asymptomatic individuals.*
>
> **—Mayo Clinic records, Dr. Michael Ackerman notes, September 23, 2003**

Dr. Ackerman recommends 20 milligrams of beta blocker per day for one month, then 40 milligrams per day. The beta blocker will prevent Delaney's heart from beating beyond two-thirds capacity and thus, in theory, greatly lessen the potential for an "episode." There are major side effects, which include loss of energy and constant physical and emotional fatigue. Depression is also a side effect, although not directly from the beta blocker but instead from the impact it has on the individual's ability to function.

Regardless, Delaney will begin the beta blockers the next day. For the following 2,555 days she will take the beta blocker each morning, never once missing a single dose. Her heart will not beat beyond two-thirds capacity, and in conjunction she will function with two-thirds the energy and stamina of her peers.

But what about sports and physical activity? Cathy and I talk with Dr. Ackerman about Delaney's personality, and about how sports and competition are a major aspect of who and what she is. We ask about statistics and percentages—in essence, probabilities that she will ever have an episode, given that she has never had one to date and she will be taking the beta blockers daily.

Dr. Ackerman is unable to give us any answers, as there is not enough data to be able to make any predictions. We ask if she will be prohibited from running down the hallway in school or climbing a steep hill and thus raising her heart rate. How about when she gets emotional, angry or frustrated? Will she be prohibited from having emotions or will a drug be prescribed so that she becomes emotionally neutral? Finally we discuss whether, if Delaney is to be prohibited from competitive sports and from being physically active, she will need psychiatric medication and a therapist.

> We had a lengthy discussion about the current recommendations regarding competitive sports, including the formal Bethesda Conference recommendations that competitive sports should be prohibited in individuals with long QT syndrome ...
>
> I am not sure all patients with long QT syndrome should be equally penalized/restricted from sport activity. There is no doubt about the incredible psychological importance of an active lifestyle that includes

recreation and competitive sports at this age. It would seem reasonable that she could participate in her current activities.

—Mayo Clinic records, Dr. Michael Ackerman notes, September 23, 2003

Dr. Ackerman then goes on to point out that in Minnesota, athletes with long QT syndrome are prohibited from playing high school sports, and that he is one of the authors of these rules. We will cross that bridge, however, if we ever come to it.

In the meantime, he says, he will fully support Delaney continuing to compete, as long as she takes her beta blockers daily and has no episodes of dizziness or fainting. Even though Delaney is only 10, he tells her that while she has never had even a symptom, if a first episode happens it could be fatal. He emphasizes that it is essential she understand this, and that it is her life that is at risk.

As the three of us drive home to Minneapolis, Delaney's sobs subside and she falls asleep. What thoughts are running through her head? No 10-year-old should have to be so aware of their own mortality. I cannot read her mind, but her distress and fear are palpable. Soon, however, those emotions will be replaced with anger, driven by a dauntless determination.

The road stretches out before us, and as I drive I realize that once again I am looking into the abyss. And once again it is looking back at me.

Chapter 14

Cathy and I concur that Delaney should continue to be able to participate in competitive sports. We recognize that taking this away from her would have an extraordinarily negative impact on her emotional well-being and stability. She cannot go from who and what she is to becoming extremely physically limited because of a diagnosis for which she has never once had a single episode. But before coming to a final decision we ask Delaney's grandfather, Dr. John Middlebrook, what he thinks. He is a specialist in internal medicine and was chief of staff at a prominent Twin Cities hospital. He has researched long QT syndrome thoroughly, especially regarding asymptomatic individuals.

His conclusion is that there is no data to support denying Delaney the ability to continue with competitive sports. He emphasizes that there is no measurable risk factor for asymptomatic individuals, that any risk is very low, that the rules and regulations in place stem from an overabundance of caution. He is also very familiar with his granddaughter. To take away from her an essential element of her being has the strong potential of causing harm to her emotionally and psychologically, in his mind a greater likelihood than the unknown but small chance of her having an episode and dying on the ice. Although it seems a difficult choice, it really is not. Delaney must be allowed to live, even if there is a risk that comes with it. So, Delaney will continue to compete.

She begins another hockey season, her seventh, in October 2003. She will skate for the Washburn Squirt A team and I will again be her coach. Ali and Jill will join her on the team, but we'll lose Nicole, who has moved with her family to White Bear Lake.

Delaney is now a fifth grader at St. Paul Academy, her first year at SPA. She is asked to tell her new classmates some things about herself.

One of the things she tells them about is her long QT diagnosis and the medication she takes daily. Cathy and I have already informed SPA so that they are aware.

For Delaney, the impact of 40 milligrams of beta blockers daily is extreme and obvious. During fall soccer she is listless and has difficulty even running. It will be her last season of travel soccer. She will continue to play for SPA's school team, but that too will end when she is in eighth grade. Although she is perpetually exhausted she does well enough in school, but the amount of focus and effort this requires is significant.

It is in the cold of the hockey rink that she feels the best, the most energetic. She steps out of the zombie existence imposed by the beta blockers and becomes fully alive again, even if only for an hour and operating at two-thirds the energy and endurance of the other skaters.

Delaney also adapts her play to overcome her physical limitations. As a defender she begins to recognize and understand the pattern of the game, how to use the ice and her skills to overcome her lack of endurance and energy. The magazine *Let's Play Hockey* publishes an article on the "10 Golden Rules for Defense." She cuts the article out and hangs it on her bedroom wall. She increases the physicality of her play, particularly in front of her net. She does more than merely survive her first year on high-dose beta blockers.

Chapter 15

Delaney, Cathy and I return to Dr. Ackerman at the Mayo Clinic in May 2004. She has not seen him since the previous September, when she was placed on the 40 milligrams of beta blocker. We discuss how Delaney has been since the previous visit.

> She continues to be asymptomatic and takes the beta blockers at 40 milligrams regularly [daily].
>
> They have noticed an extreme negative effect on her endurance and activity level.
>
> An exercise test was performed ... her heart rate only increased to 115 beats per minute. [The average for an 11 -year-old girl is 180 beats per minute.]
>
> In fact, I think we may have overmedicated her ... thus I think we may have exceeded the desired effect of the beta blocker and exchanged it with rather prominent endurance limitations and fatiguability.

—Mayo Clinic records, Dr. Michael Ackerman notes, May 27, 2004

Dr. Ackerman acknowledges that the 40 milligrams of beta blocker daily is too much, and the negative impact on Delaney's overall well-being is unacceptable. He reduces the beta blocker to 30 milligrams daily.

He then discusses with us Delaney's ongoing participation in competitive sports. He continues to approve but again emphasizes that she will be prohibited from competing in sports in high school, per the Minnesota guidelines that he himself authored.

Dr. Ackerman doesn't say so, but he seems to be internally grappling with what is actually known about long QT syndrome and what is simply overcautious speculation. We don't know it yet, but Dr. Ackerman is in the process of altering his opinion about whether athletes with the diagnosis should be prohibited from competing in high school sports in Minnesota.

IV. Playing With the Girls

Chapter 16

At 30 milligrams of beta blocker per day Delaney's perpetual exhaustion is lessened, but it's still there, a daily obstacle in all that she does. But there is a positive difference that she can feel, and that Cathy and I can see. Thirty milligrams seems to be the balance point between safety and ability to function.

In the 2004-05 season, 11-year-old Delaney, now a sixth grader, moves from playing with the boys to playing on a girls' team, the Washburn U12 A's. The majority of the team is composed of 12-year-old seventh-graders. They are good athletes and good skaters, but none have skated during the off-season or gone to spring and fall hockey clinics or hockey camps. None have played off-season AAA hockey. They play hockey only during the hockey season, from late October to mid-March. The rest of the year they play other sports and do other things. In other words they have slightly less hockey experience than Delaney up to this point.

Delaney is also dealing with another major transition. After seven years, she will no longer be coached by me. Now, instead, I'll be the head coach of our son Ian's Pee Wee A team.

The U12 A team and Delaney have a difficult season. They are not playing in District One, instead they are the sole U12 A team from Minneapolis, They play in a conference with North St. Paul, Irondale, Forest Lake and the state U12 A power, White Bear Lake. White Bear Lake is loaded. Their top player is Hannah Brandt, a future All-American at the University of Minnesota and 2018 Olympic Gold Medal winner. She and her teammates exist in a hockey culture that emphasizes being the best and winning. The White Bear Lake players all play hockey year round. Skating for that team is Nicole, Delaney's longtime teammate with Washburn.

Although the Washburn girls give their best all season, the skill difference between them and the teams they face is striking. White Bear Lake beats them 12-1 in one of the games, the total shots on goal are 35-3. The Washburn parents cheer when their girls are able to bring the puck past the center-ice line and into the White Bear Lake zone. The Washburn parents, however, are never anything but positive and upbeat during the season. The same is true with their daughters, and as result the team chemistry is solid. Delaney receives many compliments about how tough she is around the Washburn goal, which is where most of her ice time during games is spent.

White Bear Lake and Nicole will win the Minnesota State U12 A Championship in March 2005. The final season record for Washburn U12 A, meanwhile, is 5-35. Delaney sums up her feelings about the season for Cathy and me: "I like all the girls on the team," she says. "It was fun being on a team with them, and they're good friends." But, she adds, "I don't want to play on that weak of a team again if I don't have to."

Chapter 17

Delaney is coming to the end of her competitive soccer-playing days. She has difficulty running without becoming exhausted, especially when the weather Is warm.

In the spring of 2005, at 12 years old, Delaney plays softball for the SPA girls' sixth-grade team. The pitcher, Sami Fox, is also only 12, but she is already 5 feet 9 inches tall. Sami has been a travel softball player since she was 8. She has a private pitching instructor. In three years, as a 15-year-old ninth-grader at SPA, she will be named to the Minnesota High School All-State team.

In the spring of 2005 Sami Fox is unhittable against other 11- and 12-year-olds. The problem is, who will be her catcher? Her pitches come so fast and with such movement that she is almost uncatchable.

Delaney volunteers to be the catcher. She must learn how to handle Sami's grown-up pitches. Yes, the pitches will occasionally miss her glove and strike her in the shin guards, chest guard or right in the middle of her catcher's mask, always with a loud "thwack." The pitches come in so fast that often the ball will rebound directly back to Sami on the pitching mound. The ball will also occasionally strike Delaney in the arm or the thigh where, by the next day, a massive bruise will have formed. Not once does she cry.

SPA wins the league championship, but softball does not become the athletic void-filler for soccer for Delaney. Instead, it is hockey. More hockey. Spring, summer, fall hockey.

We have heard about off-season AAA girls' hockey, but Cathy and I have no idea how to find a U12 AAA team for Delaney. But we do have someone to ask: Nicole's parents, Jeff and Gayle. They are not able to get Delaney onto Nicole's AAA team, the Wild, not only because no spots are available, but also because Delaney has not yet proven herself good enough. But Jeff and Gayle do connect us with a new AAA team being formed from players in the northwest suburbs, primarily Andover and Coon Rapids. The team is called the Ice Phantoms, and they need another skater.

Spring practices are at night, 25 miles from our home in south Minneapolis. Delaney does homework in the car on the drive to and from the arena. The Ice Phantoms play in several prominent U12 weekend tournaments during the summer, which take place primarily at the rinks at the Blaine Sports Complex. They don't win any tournaments, but they do win games. It is a new hockey experience for Delaney and for Cathy and me, this summer-tournament, AAA-hockey scene. Delaney loves it. Playing at a higher skill and competitive level she visibly improves. The door has opened for her to a whole new world of hockey.

Gayle and Jeff also introduce Delaney to a summer hockey training program, run by 27-year-old women's hockey icon Winny Brodt, Minnesota's first Ms. Hockey (the top high school player in the state) and a U.S. National Team fixture. Her program is called OS. It focuses on skating and stickhandling drills and off-ice agility and speed training. Delaney spends several weeks in the OS program and improves significantly. Of far greater import, she makes a positive impression with her determination and desire, and Winny, as coach, mentor and advocate, will become a paramount influence on Delaney's evolution as a hockey player.

Chapter 18

In the fall of 2005 Delaney is a 12-year-old, 4-11, 95-pound seventh-grader at St. Paul Academy. She continues to take her beta blocker every morning and endure its side effects of physical and mental exhaustion. Consequently, if she doesn't have sports or other activities after school, she will take a nap. Bedtime comes early, and there is never an issue with her falling asleep. In essence, she has to work much harder than her peers each day to keep up with school and sports. Cathy and I both alter our work schedules to make it easier for Delaney to rest after school. We find a routine that works, and Delaney carries on as a solid B-plus student at SPA.

After a summer of AAA hockey and training with Winny Brodt, Delaney is a much better player than the previous season. She does not want to play U12 A for Washburn again. She does not want to experience another 5-35 season, nor does she want to play on a team of girls brand-new to hockey. She is one of only a couple girls returning to the U12 A team, as the majority of the players from the previous year have aged up to U14. The girls who will make up the U12 team for 2005-06 have limited hockey experience, many having started hockey in the Washburn program only within the last two years, with some coming directly from Minneapolis park teams.

However, District One, the combination of Minneapolis and St. Paul youth hockey, has plans for Delaney. This is particularly true for the director of girls' hockey in District One, whom we'll call Joan. Joan explains to me how important it is to girls' hockey in Minneapolis that Washburn have a U12 A team, and one that is at least semi-competitive. She tells me that Delaney is a key to that—she should not play Pee Wee boys' hockey, nor should she try to move up to the District One U14 team. Instead she, and Cathy and I, should focus our efforts and our loyalty on the good of Minneapolis girls' hockey, regardless of what impact this could have on Delaney. Joan initially presents this as something for Delaney and us to consider, an option. But within weeks, during tryouts, she dispels any illusion that there is a choice.

Washburn youth hockey tryouts begin in October. I have been asked to coach the Washburn Bantam A team, where Ian will be playing. Delaney announces her intention to try out for the District One U14 A team that Joan is in charge of. Ali also will be trying out for the team, even though she is also U12 age. The tryouts are at Parade Ice Gardens. On one rink is the U14 tryout. On the other is the Pee Wee tryout. Before Delaney and Ali take the ice for the U14 tryout, Joan comes up to me and says that Delaney can only try out if I agree that if she doesn't make the U14 A team that she will instead skate for the U14 B team. She cannot play for any other team, including the Pee Wee team. Joan then presents me with a document she has drawn up that states these terms and tells me if I do not sign she will immediately pull Delaney off the ice. She presents Ali's father, Stan, with the same option and the same document.

I respond, calmly, that I can't sign this document as I don't agree with either its terms or the motivation behind it. I am now quite certain that no matter how well Delaney performs at the U14 tryouts she will not make the A team. Stan is not so calm. He becomes quite angry and shouts in Joan's face that she has no concern for the individual girls and will sacrifice them to make herself look good in the eyes of Minnesota hockey. Joan's response is to come directly back to me and place her face inches from mine, yelling that she does care about all the girls and that Stan is wrong. I tell her that I never accused her of not caring about the girls, but I still would not be signing the document. Joan then walks to the gate leading to the ice, opens it, stops the tryout and tells Delaney and Ali to leave the ice immediately. They both skate toward the gate as the girls and coaches on the ice, and the parents in the stands, watch in silence.

Delaney and Ali then walk through the lobby to the other Parade rink, where the Pee Wee tryout is taking place. They step onto the

ice, where Delaney will stay for the weeklong tryout, but the next day Ali returns to the U12 team. The Pee Wee tryouts end on the same day as the Bantam tryouts. I know where Delaney has finished in the Pee Wee tryout rankings, because I know the evaluators—they're the same evaluators I use for the Bantam tryouts—and they have ranked Delaney seventh among the Pee Wee skaters.

But somehow, she is not picked for the Pee Wee A team. Regardless of her ability it appears she lost her standing among the boys when she played the previous year for the U12 team. In addition, there appears to be some payback for the years I picked girls over boys for the Squirt teams I coached.

Delaney receives the call on the Saturday morning after tryouts have ended. She is on the Pee Wee B team. She is devastated and sits in the corner of the dining room, sobbing. Within days the Pee Wee B team plays their first scrimmage, the first of four in six days. Delaney, who has been named a team captain, has clearly benefited from her summer hockey, and is the best defense player on the ice in each of the four scrimmages. The wheels of destiny are turning, however, and four games will be the full sum of her Pee Wee hockey career

ice, where Delaney will stay for the weeklong tryout, but the next day Ali returns to the U12 team. The Pee Wee tryouts end on the same day as the Bantam tryouts. I know where Delaney has finished in the Pee Wee tryout rankings, because I know the evaluators—they're the same evaluators I use for the Bantam tryouts—and they have ranked Delaney seventh among the Pee Wee skaters.

But somehow, she is not picked for the Pee Wee A team. Regardless of her ability it appears she lost her standing among the boys when she played the previous year for the U12 team. In addition, there appears to be some payback for the years I picked girls over boys for the Squirt teams I coached.

Delaney receives the call on the Saturday morning after tryouts have ended. She is on the Pee Wee B team. She is devastated and sits in the corner of the dining room, sobbing. Within days the Pee Wee B team plays their first scrimmage, the first of four in six days. Delaney, who has been named a team captain, has clearly benefited from her summer hockey, and is the best defense player on the ice in each of the four scrimmages. The wheels of destiny are turning, however, and four games will be the full sum of her Pee Wee hockey career

ice, where Delaney will stay for the weeklong tryout, but the next day Ali returns to the U12 team. The Pee Wee tryouts end on the same day as the Bantam tryouts. I know where Delaney has finished in the Pee Wee tryout rankings, because I know the evaluators—they're the same evaluators I use for the Bantam tryouts—and they have ranked Delaney seventh among the Pee Wee skaters.

But somehow, she is not picked for the Pee Wee A team. Regardless of her ability it appears she lost her standing among the boys when she played the previous year for the U12 team. In addition, there appears to be some payback for the years I picked girls over boys for the Squirt teams I coached.

Delaney receives the call on the Saturday morning after tryouts have ended. She is on the Pee Wee B team. She is devastated and sits in the corner of the dining room, sobbing. Within days the Pee Wee B team plays their first scrimmage, the first of four in six days. Delaney, who has been named a team captain, has clearly benefited from her summer hockey, and is the best defense player on the ice in each of the four scrimmages. The wheels of destiny are turning, however, and four games will be the full sum of her Pee Wee hockey career

Chapter 19

We were told at the very first consultation with Dr. Ackerman in 2003 that yes, he would approve of Delaney continuing to play competitive sports, if she took the daily beta blockers. When she reached high school, however, she would no longer be able to play. The Minnesota State High School League specifically banned students with the long QT syndrome diagnosis from competing in high school sports. Dr. Ackerman himself had helped author this rule. Each time Delaney had a follow up with him, Dr. Ackerman, after asking how her sports were going, would again mention the long QT ban for high school athletes.

Perhaps it was simply my curiosity that led me to suggest to Delaney that she attend the first tryout for the girls' varsity hockey team, St. Paul United. It was also likely my knowledge that she had never experienced a single heart episode in her life. It might even have been the call I received from Kevin McMullen, a coach of the Novas, the Minneapolis girls' high school varsity team, inviting Delaney to play for his team while informing me that as a Minneapolis resident and middle school student at SPA, she was eligible to do so.

St. Paul United is a co-op team between St. Paul Academy and the Convent of the Visitation High School. The team and the co-op had been in existence since 1994-95, the first year that girls' high school hockey teams competed in Minnesota. The practices and the home games are at Drake Arena, on the St. Paul Academy campus. The first tryout was a Monday night in early November 2005. Delaney had played a Pee Wee B game the day before, but that Monday night was free from game or practice. Yes, she wanted to skate at the tryout. She thought about it some more and Yes! she really wanted to. Cathy and I discussed it and we both felt there was no harm in seeing how

Delaney would measure up against the much older United girls. We had no idea how good the players or the team was. Even though Ian was in his fourth year at SPA and Delaney her third, we had never seen a United game, and only one SPA boys' game.

I drove Delaney to the tryout. She said she was nervous. "Nothing to be nervous about," I assured her. "Do your best. Have a good experience."

We went into the arena together and I introduced her to the team coach, whom I had previously met once. I then went to sit in the stands for the hourlong session. Other high school teams might not allow parents to attend the tryouts, but not so St. Paul United, and I wasn't the only parent there. Delaney, at 12, was not only the youngest player on the ice, she was also the smallest. By the end of the hour it was also clear to me that she was one of the best and quickest skaters.

As we drove home Delaney told me how much fun she had skating with United. She asked me how she looked in comparison to the other girls. "You looked good," I told her. "I'm glad it was a good experience and you had fun." When we arrived home, Delaney went upstairs to her room. Cathy then tells me that while we were driving home the United coach called, asking to talk to me.

"What do you think he wants to talk about?" she wonders.

"I believe he wants to talk to me about Delaney playing for the United varsity team."

"Really? She must have looked good."

"She did."

I call the coach back. "I want her on the team," he says. "I'll even buy her a white helmet myself."

I convey what the coach has said to Cathy. She is excited, but she remembers. "She isn't allowed to play high school sports—Dr. Ackerman has told us that many times. How could she possibly be allowed to play?"

I respond by running through the logic that has gotten us this far. "According to the medical rules and guidelines for people diagnosed with long QT syndrome, she is not supposed to play competitive

sports or exert herself in any form or manner. She is supposed to be sedentary—in essence, physically stifled, a girl living in a bubble. Yet the doctor who wrote these rules has consistently allowed her to continue living a normal life, to continue being an athlete, to continue being a competitor. He has not only allowed her to do this, he has encouraged her and congratulated her for it. What's the difference between playing Washburn Pee Wee boy's hockey and St. Paul United girls' high school hockey that would alter Dr. Ackerman's medical opinion?"

"There is no difference," Cathy replies. "There's no difference that would justify keeping Delaney from playing for United. There is only the high school rule, and according to it she can't play high school hockey, now or ever."

We agree that Delaney will attend the second tryout set for the next night. We also agree that I will call my father, Dr. John Middlebrook, to ask his opinion. But I already know what it will be: that Delaney should play for United.

Chapter 20

St. Paul United has additional tryouts on Tuesday and Wednesday nights. Delaney skates at both, and is chosen to be among the top two defense pairs on the United varsity. But the Minnesota State High School League wouldn't allow her to play, no matter how nicely we ask, no matter how forcefully we demand. Delaney's diagnosis of long QT syndrome trumps everything.

But first the MSHSL will have to find out, and we don't intend to tell them. St. Paul Academy knows of Delaney's diagnosis, or at least they once knew. When Delaney entered SPA in fifth grade we informed the school of her diagnosis and that she was taking beta blockers. Delaney even gave a presentation to her fifth-grade class about her diagnosis. Delaney has succeeded so well in her quest to be normal that by November 2005, SPA has forgotten she even has the diagnosis.

One major hurdle remains, however, before Delaney can skate for United. She, like all varsity athletes, needs a complete physical, and both Mayo and her pediatric clinic, Metro Peds, will automatically disqualify her from competing because of her diagnosis. This is where Delaney's grandfather steps in. He arranges her physical with one of his medical colleagues. The doctor giving the physical notes that not only is Delaney a healthy 12-year-old, she is one of the strongest he has ever examined. The doctor's report makes no mention of long QT syndrome, and so she is cleared to skate for St. Paul United for the 2005-06 high school season. Every year, for the next five years, the same doctor clears her to play, never once mentioning long QT syndrome.

Delaney will play her first varsity game in the middle of November. But first, Cathy, Ian, Delaney and I have a family meeting, to establish that none of us of us can ever tell anyone else about Delaney's diagnosis—not teammates or coaches, not friends, not anyone. It must remain a secret among the four of us, Grandpa John and Grandma Phyllis. If we tell anyone the secret, Delaney is done with hockey, done with competitive sports. The most impressive secret keeper will turn out to be Ian. He is a 14-year-old eighth-grader at the time. Surely at some point over the next five-plus years he can't help but tell someone. But he never does, not once.

It might be very easy for others at this point to believe they could judge our family—Cathy and I as parents, grandfather John as the doctor who arranged Delaney's physicals—and disapprove, even revile. How could we risk Delaney's life just for hockey?

But we didn't see it this way. What we saw was a girl who from her earliest existence showed she was born to be a competitor, an athlete, a warrior. By age 10 her self-identity was firmly established, but then she receives a diagnosis of a heart condition ominously known as "Sudden Death Syndrome," a diagnosis not based on any symptoms or episodes she has ever had, but rather based entirely upon EKG testing. The diagnosis demands that she shut down all strenuous physical activity, bans her from competitive sports, consigns her to live a compromised life. Yet even her doctor at the Mayo Clinic, a world expert in long QT syndrome, agrees that there is no actual testing or data to justify such an extreme reaction to the diagnosis. In essence, the rules and restrictions are based upon a better-safe-than-sorry premise. In the meantime, Delaney and her ability to be the person she was born to be, is to be sacrificed in the name of caution.

The sister who came before her, Annalise, who fought so hard to live but had no chance, would want Delaney to live completely, to be what she was born to be. Cathy and I would not stop Delaney from living, would not accept a better-safe-than-sorry life for her. Dr. Ackerman agreed with us when he allowed her to continue playing competitive sports.

We didn't care what others thought, and we still don't care. We made the right choice for Delaney.

Chapter 21

Girls' hockey is a major high school sport in Minnesota. More than 135 girls' high school teams compete in the 2005-06 season. With an average of 18 players per team, that's more than 1,320 girls playing. But only a handful are 12-year-old seventh-graders.

St. Paul United, the co-op between St. Paul Academy and the Convent of the Visitation, is in the Minnesota small-school bracket, Class A. The bigger schools skate in the Class AA bracket. United, in existence since 1994-95, the first year of girls' high school hockey in Minnesota, have consistently finished at or around .500. They have never been to the state tournament and no United played has skated in D1 college hockey since the late '90s; only a few have played D3. Over the years, the vast majority of United players have never skated outside the high school season. From a win/lose standpoint they are the very definition of mediocrity. We are unaware of any of this history during Delaney's first season with United, but even if we were, we would not have cared. We and Delaney are simply thrilled that she is able to compete at a level that matches her ability and determination.

In addition to Delaney, United has two eighth-graders and two ninth-graders, with the rest being upper-class students, several of whom are six years older than her. They treat Delaney like a cherished little sister, completely welcoming her into the chemistry of the team. The Herzog, Quinlan, Ruhland and Walston families, the hockey-playing daughters and their parents in particular, welcome Delaney, Cathy and me and in doing so become friends for life.

Delaney is still only 4 foot 11; her defense partner is a 6-foot-tall, 17-year-old junior. United skates only four defense, so Delaney is out for every other shift. In some games United are overwhelmed by their opponents, particularly state powerhouse Blake, unable to get the puck out of their zone for minutes at a time, even when a United forward has the puck two feet from the blue line and no opponent within 10 feet of her. In some games they are unable to contain teams that have an individual high-skilled player. In other games, however, against opponents of a comparable level, the United players show effort and determination. The culmination is an outdoor game with archrival Minneapolis, won by United, 4-1.

During the season Delaney is also overwhelmed at times. She has no offensive highlights, although she does, so to speak, break the ice with a single assist. But she announces and asserts herself on the blue line against individual opponents that the other United skaters have difficulty countering. For example, the St. Paul Blades have a skater who will score over 60 points that season, but Delaney, focused entirely on stopping her, holds her scoreless.

The season ends with a three-overtime loss to Richfield in the first round of the playoffs. The United players emerge from the dressing room sobbing, all because their seasons, and for some their careers, are over. Delaney also has tears streaming down her cheeks; she is overcome not only by her own emotions but also by those of her teammates. But her tears are also tears of fulfillment and accomplishment. At 12 years of age she has truly earned her varsity letter, realizing a dream that did not even exist four months earlier. The next day we order her St. Paul Academy letter jacket with the 2005-06 hockey patch that will go on the left sleeve. When she, Cathy and I go to the girls high school state tournament two weeks later, the letter jacket, together with her pride in wearing it, fit perfectly.

V. An Impossible Dream

Chapter 22

Delaney, having turned 13 on March 30, 1993, is now a U14 player. The Ice Phantoms AAA team has been disbanded, so she goes to an open tryout in the early spring, supposedly designed to find teams for worthy players. Apparently no one considers her worthy, and she receives no offers to play. We sign her up for Winny Brodt's summer OS program, which takes place three days a week. But no AAA team, no tournaments and no games.

Fortunately, the boys' coach at SPA, the former NHL defenseman Craig Norwich, is an entrepreneur. In conjunction with a wealthy sponsor he forms his own AAA club for boys and girls, the Minnesota Rockets. Ian will play for the Rockets' 16-year-old boys' team, in preparation for playing varsity hockey at SPA for Norwich the coming season. Delaney joins the Rockets, first as a U14 player, but she is soon moved to the U16 team based on her level of play.

The Rockets U16 girls are on a low tier competitively. They do not win a game in any of the tournaments they compete in. Yet with the combination of their games and the practices run by Norwich, together with the Winny Brodt OS training, Delaney continues to improve. More important, she looks forward to the ice times and the dry land training. Not once does she say she doesn't want to go because she is tired or doesn't feel good, even though we know she is often beta-blocker tired and not feeling good. There is nothing else she would rather do at this point in her life than play hockey.

On June 6, 2006 Delaney, Cathy and I see Dr. Ackerman a third time, a little more than a year since her last visit. We decide to not put him in the awkward position of knowing she has played high school varsity hockey the previous season.

Ms. Delaney Middlebrook continues to be a delightful asymptomatic 13-year-old.

She has successfully completed seventh grade as a straight-A student.

She remains extremely active in hockey and softball.

It is amazing how much she has grown in the last two years.

—Mayo Clinic records, Dr. Michael Ackerman notes, June 6, 2006

Dr. Ackerman further notes that Delaney has done extremely well at 30 milligrams of beta blockers per day and that she seems to be at the maximum tolerated dose. Her heartbeat maxes at 129 beats per minute on the stress test, only two-thirds the capacity of her peers. He again approves of her continued participation in competitive sports but states that in the name of "extreme caution" we should carry an external defibrillator with us, even as he also relates that there has not been a single need for use of a defibrillator by any of his patients. We do not tell him that doing so would spell the end of her high school sports career, as it would bring her long QT diagnosis out in the open. But at every arena, we make a point of locating where the defibrillator is. We have already bought one and donated it as a gift to SPA and Drake Arena.

The summer of 2006 also brings for Delaney and her United teammates their first experience of international hockey. I lived in Sweden for two years and have many connections there. Together with the help of a Swede, Magnus Sköld (also the godfather to our son, Ian), we arrange a one-week hockey trip to Stockholm in late July. In addition to four games against Swedish teams with get-togethers after each one, the players and their parents experience all that a Stockholm summer has to offer, including a boat ride through the Stockholm archipelago, visits to museums, a Swedish youth disco and experiencing a sun that is up most of the night. Two of the games are against AIK, the famed sports club founded in 1891. The players meet the Swedish goaltender Kim Martin, who won an NCAA title at Minnesota-Duluth and was the hero of the 2006 Swedish women's Olympic silver medal team that beat the heavily favored Americans in the semifinals.

The Stockholm trip is an experience that no other U.S. high school girls' hockey team has ever had before.

In the fall Winny and OS send both a U16 and a U19 team to compete in a tournament at Shattuck Prep School in Fairbault. Winny picks Delaney to skate for the OS U16 team. Delaney is thrilled; Cathy and I are surprised. At 13 she will be the youngest player in the tournament. Yes, she has improved immensely over the summer, but there is nothing about her hockey abilities that sets her apart. Perhaps it's her drive and determination that Winny sees and decides to reward by putting Delaney on the team. In doing so, she has opened the door for Delaney, giving her the chance to skate with high-level players in select competition. Delaney rises to the challenge and plays well enough to show she belongs. She skates over the threshold into a higher hockey sphere and will never look back.

On the opening night of the competition I see Joan, the girls' hockey director for District One. The last time I saw her was the previous October, when Joan removed Delaney from the ice during the U14 tryouts. That night at Shattuck Joan puts a great deal of effort into avoiding me, but I do see her frenetically searching though the rosters in the tournament program to see who it is that Delaney is skating for.

Chapter 23

The 2006-07 season is Delaney's eighth-grade year and her second season skating for the St. Paul United varsity. Three additional eighth-graders join United to replace the seniors who have graduated. It is a positive season, much like the previous one, as United finishes with close to a .500 record.

Delaney has grown to 5 foot 1 and tops 100 pounds for the first time. She continues to play strong defense but has yet to add a meaningful offensive element to her game, other than she has quick hands that allow her to shoot the puck with some authority from the point. She scores her first high school goal during a holiday tournament in Rochester.

When the season is over Delaney announces to me that she has set two goals for herself as a hockey player. The first is to someday be named to the All-State girls' high school team as one of six defenders chosen by the Minnesota high school varsity hockey coaches from the state's 600 eligible blueliners. Her second goal is to play Division 1 college hockey. No United player has been All-State or played Division 1 for many years.

There is nothing that I have seen from Delaney, other than off-the-charts determination, to indicate she would ever achieve either goal. They seem to be better described as dreams—impossible dreams, that Cathy and I know will not come true. Besides, I can't see how she could ever overcome the severe limitations imposed by her daily beta blockers. Her goals may not be as unrealistic as Ian in fourth grade telling me hasn't decided whether he will play pro baseball for the Minnesota Twins or pro hockey for the Minnesota Wild. But I am supportive and encouraging, just as I was with Ian.

Thanks to the high-level OS training and opportunities provided by Winny Brodt, Delaney has advanced enough to be asked by Jeff and Gayle to play for Nicole's team, the Wild, in the coming offseason. The Wild is a good U14 AAA team, but they win games, not tournaments. Either way, Delaney and Nicole are reunited on the ice, and Jeff and Gayle with Cathy and me in the stands. It is not like old times in Washburn youth hockey. It is much better.

At a spring weekend tournament I watch another AAA team, the Blades, dominate in each of their games. I recognize Hannah and Marissa Brandt from White Bear Lake, Sami Reber from Edina and Rachel Ramsey from Minnetonka, but I do not know who the other players are. Gayle tells me that their coach has put together a team with most of the best U14 players in the metro area. The result is a powerful unit, but also one that inspires extreme dislike from other teams and their parents.

The summer of 2007 and United again goes international, this time on a trip to Helsinki, Finland, again arranged by Magnus and myself. And again the trip is more than just hockey. It includes a visit to the Finnish Parliament and also to a copper mine outside Helsinki. Joining United are two former United skaters who are playing D3 hockey for Minnesota colleges. On the rink, United wins all four games. But even more noteworthy for Cathy and me is that Delaney crosses a hockey threshold and adds offensive skills to her strong defense play, scoring five goals in the four games. The coach of the Finland women's national team watches one of the games and afterward awards Delaney a prize as the best player on the ice.

As Delaney continues to improve as a hockey player she also continues to have zero tolerance for bullies and those who try to intimidate. In August 2007 she plays on a team in the Midwest Selects tournament. In a close game she and her teammates endure a player on the opposing team who is more focused on cheap, even dirty, play when the referee's eyes are somewhere else. With 30 seconds left in the game, Delaney's team scores to increase their lead to 3-1. Delaney and her teammate's nemesis are on the ice for the final seconds. With 10 seconds remaining Delaney gives the bully a full-force cross-check to the mask, sending her crashing to the ice. "Two minutes well worth it," Delaney tells me when she emerges from the dressing room. In the meantime, six different parents of Delaney's teammates have come to me, shaking my hand, giving me a hug, telling me they absolutely love what Delaney did.

Chapter 24

Delaney, Cathy and I see Dr. Ackerman again in the summer of 2007. It proves to be a momentous meeting: he learns that Delaney has been a varsity athlete for two years, in direct contradiction to Minnesota high school rules.

> *Delaney continues to be a most delightful 14-year-old young woman who has just graduated from eighth grade.*
>
> *She is growing up most beautifully.*
>
> *She has A's and B-pluses for grades.*
>
> *She continues to be symptom-free from a long QT standpoint.*
>
> —Mayo Clinic records, Dr. Michael Ackerman notes, June 13, 2007

Dr. Ackerman writes that Delaney entering puberty as she continues to play hockey and softball could increase her risk level, but there has been no significant change in her QT interval. Although her peak heart rate it still only 129 beats per minute, her aerobic fitness is in the highest levels for her age group. He again says that Delaney is still at risk for sudden death because of her long QT condition, but emphasizes, "Delaney and her family have thought through these issues carefully and with 'eyes wide open'." Translated into everyday English, Dr. Ackerman is acknowledging that because Delaney has had no symptoms or episodes, either before taking beta blockers or after, she should be able to continue competing—but that the ultimate responsibility for this decision is ours, not his.

Dr. Ackerman also asks Delaney if her softball season is just starting up. When she tells him softball has just ended he asks her, "Did you play high school softball?"

"Yes, I did, for the JV," Delaney responds.

Dr. Ackerman looks at Cathy and me. We then tell him that she also played varsity hockey the previous two school years. He does not ask us how this could have occurred. He mentions the Bethesda Conference Guidelines, which prohibit Delaney from playing high school sports, but doesn't challenge or argue against her competing as a high school athlete. If anything, Dr. Ackerman appears amused, and he nods at Delaney in supportive affirmation.

Dr. Ackerman does request, for extreme caution's sake, that Delaney try returning to 40 milligrams per day of beta blocker, just to see how she responds. We agree, and for two weeks Delaney increases from 30 milligrams to 40. The result is the same as when she was previously taking the 40 milligrams: extreme physical and mental exhaustion, with accompanying depression. And so she returns to 30 milligrams per day.

VI. An Extraordinary Ascent

Chapter 25

During the 2007-08 season, Delaney's ninth-grade year at SPA, her transformation as an athlete and a hockey player takes place almost overnight. She adds offensive ability to already strong defensive skills. She is visibly quicker, particularly in her lateral movement. She carries the puck with confidence, stickhandles through and around opposing players with sure hands and sure feet. On a low-scoring United team she finishes with two goals and eight assists while remaining a shutdown defender, the most noticeable player on the rink.

Cathy and I have no explanation for Delaney's great leap forward on the ice. Yes, she has had significant high-level training with Winny Brodt and high-level AAA competition during the off season, and she showed flashes of excellence in Finland. But even so, we can't get over how much she has improved. To us it seems impossible.

Highland Park Ice Arena in St. Paul is located only blocks from St. Paul Academy. Dianne Ness has been running a skating clinic for hockey players out of Highland for many years. Her instructors have included her son Andy. Each session lasted 30 minutes and focused on all aspects of hockey skating—forward, backward, turns, crossovers, transitions, edging—all with the skater in full hockey gear stickhandling a puck. Delaney begins this training with Andy Ness in late March 2008. The twice-a-week sessions run from 6:45 a.m. to 7:15 a.m. This gives Delaney enough time, with me driving, to stop at Bruegger's or Jamba Juice before arriving at SPA, where classes began at 8.

Delaney also played her first season of varsity softball for SPA. In her first game she went in at left field as a defensive replacement. She started the second game and got to hit for the first time. By late April her batting average was well over .400. On a Tuesday morning skating training with Andy Ness at Highland I opened up the sports page of the St. Paul *Pioneer Press*. In the high school softball statistics Delaney was eighth in the metro area in batting average.

That same April, Minnesota Hockey holds statewide tryouts for players born in 1993 in the first step toward determining which Minnesota players will be sent to the USA U15 National Camp. There are eight girls' hockey districts in Minnesota, with each choosing 20 players to represent their individual district. After those eight district teams compete against one another in a three-day competition, Minnesota Hockey will choose 60 skaters to attend the final state tryouts in Mankato in June, from which nine forwards and six defenders will be sent to the USA Hockey U15 National Camp in Rochester, N.Y., in July.

Delaney is joined on the District One team by other players from the Twin Cities, including a St. Paul defender named Milica McMillen, who as a seventh grader at Breck School was one of the best players in the state (she will eventually become an All-American and a national champion at the University of Minnesota).

In the weekend competition District One plays three games. They lose each one and are outscored by a cumulative 22-3. Milica , however, is clearly one of the best players on any of the eight teams. Delaney, meanwhile, is a plus-3; she is on the ice for all three of District One's goals and not on for any of the 22 goals against. And she gets two assist to boot. At the end of the weekend, only five skaters from District One are invited to the Mankato Camp, including Delaney and Milica.

Chapter 26

Delaney joins a new AAA team for the spring and summer of 2008, the OS Xtreme. A step up from the Wild, it is her fourth AAA team in four summers. They recruited her after the man who runs the team, Mark Burgeson, saw her play against Breck, his daughter's high school team. The Xtreme coach is none other than Winny Brodt, so Delaney will continue to evolve under her instruction while playing in high-level AAA competition.

First, however, is the Minnesota U15 camp in Mankato. It takes place in June, not long after school is done for the year. I drive Delaney the 75 miles to Mankato where she and 60 other U15 girls will compete in a three-day-tournament ahead of the selection to go to the USA Hockey U15 National Camp in Rochester, N.Y. On the way to Mankato we stop at the campus of Gustavus Adolphus in St. Peter, where I went to college and played for the varsity hockey team. I show her a photo of me on the wall at the Gustavus Ice Arena. I am a senior with long hair and a mustache. I ask her what she thinks and she responds, "You must not have had many girlfriends when you were at Gustavus." "What?" I reply, but she is quite correct. I'm with her while she registers for the Mankato camp, but I'll have to drive back to Minneapolis that same evening. Even so I watch through an open door to the arena for five minutes before I leave. I am not the only parent doing so.

Games are played for the next three days. Parents are allowed to watch, but I have work the first two days. I come down the third morning to watch Delaney play her final game. I am told she has done very well so far. During the game I stand next to an executive for the Minnesota Wild whose daughter is also at the camp. He tells me he thinks Delaney will be selected for national camp, depending on how well she plays in the final contest. Milica McMillen's father tells me the same thing. From what I see she plays an excellent game, very strong on defense with an offensive component.

Delaney and I drive home together, and she is hopeful. She asks me what I think, and I tell her she has played well. I don't tell her the comments from the other fathers because I don't want to create false hope. "Let's keep our fingers crossed," I tell her. I then drop Delaney off at home and drive to my office to check my mail. Milica's dad has already called me at the office and left the message that the list for national camp has been posted: Delaney, together with Milica, has made it. I check online and there it is: Delaney Middlebrook, listed with five other defense players. I call Delaney. She already knows; one of the other players selected has called to tell her. Her excitement and euphoria pulse through the phone, making it vibrate in my hand. Or perhaps it is my own shaking because I am so happy. I call Cathy. She is ecstatic. Neither of us is able to do any work the rest of the afternoon; we both leave early to join Delaney at home to celebrate.

It is only a little more than two and a half years since Delaney was not allowed to try out for the U14 team, two years since no U14 AAA team thought her good enough to skate for them after an open tryout, less than five years since she began taking daily beta blockers and battling their significant side effects. Now she has become the first female from Minneapolis and the first St. Paul United player to make a USA Hockey National Camp.

We know that what Delaney is achieving is beyond extraordinary.

The U15 national camp will take place the same week in July as the third annual United international hockey trip, this time to Italy and France. There is no question which experience Delaney will choose. She'll be going to Rochester.

Chapter 27

The 2008 U15 USA Hockey National Camp runs from July 26 to August 1 at the ESL Sports Centre in suburban Rochester, N.Y. The players must pay their own way to get there, but everything else— lodging, food, ice time—is covered by USA Hockey. Six teams of 17 players each, from every hockey-playing state in the nation, are there. From the Midwest: Minnesota, Wisconsin, North Dakota, Illinois, Michigan, Indiana, Ohio. From the Northeast: Massachusetts, New York, Connecticut, New Jersey, Rhode Island, Pennsylvania. Alaska and Colorado are represented too. There are even players from non-traditional states, like Texas, Nevada, Oklahoma, California. They will train each day in the morning and afternoon, and in the evening will compete against each other. They take classes on nutrition and the psychology of winning. They get to know one another, forming connections and friendships.

Many of the players at the camp will ultimately go on to play D1 college hockey, others will play D3, and there are also those who will disappear from the hockey records before they even reach college. Being selected for the U15 national camp is no guarantee of future high-level hockey success. Many factors will come into play in the following years to determine who continues to advance and who does not. Some players, inevitably, will stop improving, often because they have physically peaked at age 15. Others will lose their motivation or simply burn out. For every player on top at age 15 there is always more than one striving to replace her. Many of the skaters are tall for 15-year-olds, 5-7 to 5-10, and weigh 130 to 150 pounds. They have perhaps impressed because of their size. At 5-3 and 110 pounds, Delaney has never impressed on that count.

I fly with Delaney to Rochester, where I'll stay in a motel and rent a car to get to the rink and back. I am one of over 70 parents who have come to Rochester to watch their daughters. Delaney and I drive from the airport to the rink, where she checks in with USA Hockey. She will play for the Gold team, together with fellow Minnesotans Karley Sylvester and Sara Carlson. The players stay in dorm rooms next to the ice complex. Delaney's roommate is a skater from Alaska. The players eat their meals in a large cafeteria attached to the dormitory. I come to the rink each day to watch training and each evening to watch the games. I also find time to drive to Niagara Falls and to swim in Lake Ontario.

The standard of play is equivalent to high-level AAA hockey, and is at least three levels above what Delaney experiences with St. Paul United. Still, Delaney shows that she belongs at the camp. She is quick, aggressive and smart on defense. Offensively she moves the puck smoothly up to her forwards. It is the most complete, exciting and fulfilling hockey week of her life. It is actually the most complete, exciting and fulfilling week of her entire life. In the meantime, Cathy is in Italy and France with the United hockey team. Although Delaney could not go, I helped to arrange the trip and Cathy has the responsibility of being team chaperone. The hockey and cultural experience she and United have in France and Italy would normally be considered incomparable, but she points out, and I agree, that it can't compare to watching our daughter skate at national camp.

The camp ends on the morning of August 1. Delaney and I join the majority of the Minnesota contingent on the flight home. The first leg of the trip is on a small plane to Chicago. As we fly over Lake Michigan we encounter a thunderstorm. A lightning bolt strikes the left wing, shutting one of the engines down. Delaney and I are already familiar with the metaphorical lightning bolt of her long QT diagnosis, that came without warning or mercy, but this our first encounter with an actual lightning bolt. The rest of the flight is white knuckle, but we survive and arrive safely in Chicago.

Chapter 28

Ten days after Delaney and I return from Rochester and Cathy from France and Italy, we head to the Mayo Clinic to see Dr. Ackerman. Delaney tells him that she was selected by USA Hockey for the U15 national camp. She describes her excitement at being selected and how amazing it was to be there with hockey girls from all over the country. Dr. Ackerman is impressed and astounded. It is clear he can't explain to himself how she could possibly be accomplishing this given the beta blockers' impact on her energy and endurance. Delaney has never been his typical long QT patient. Now, with her significant success as a hockey player, she has become divergent—an improbability.

> *I am delighted she is doing so well.*
>
> *I congratulated her on being impressively compliant with the treatment program (never once failing to take her daily medication).*
>
> *Delaney and her family have done everything they can short of removing her from the sports she loves to minimize her long QT risk.*

—Mayo Clinic records, Dr. Michael Ackerman notes, August 11, 2008

Dr. Ackerman again references the Bethesda Clinic guidelines that would have prohibited Delaney from competitive sports. But by now he no longer supports these strict guidelines. He is in a difficult position, fully supporting and celebrating Delaney, yet doing so contrary to the very rules he authored.

> *Her family is keenly aware of the issues surrounding guidelines and competitive sports recommendations, as both her parents are lawyers.*
>
> *They understand the nature of these guidelines that include the need to protect both the patient but also unfortunately sometimes the physician.*

—Mayo Clinic records, Dr. Michael Ackerman notes, August 11, 2008

By continuing to support Delaney playing competitive sports, Dr. Ackerman is choosing her well-being ... potentially at the cost of his own.

Chapter 29

In late August 2008 Delaney is skating at the Blaine Super Rink when I see Greg Brandt, whose daughter Hannah was one of the top players at the Team USA National Camp. He tells me that he was impressed with Delaney's abilities at national camp. He has recommended to Frank Mork, Coach/Leader of the Blades, that Delaney be added to the team as a defense player. This is the same U16 Blades team that dominates AAA hockey, drawing the ire of the parents of players on other teams. The next day Frank calls me to extend the offer to Delaney. He will be cutting a player from the team if Delaney says yes, so he needs to know now. I tell him I cannot decide for her, that she and Cathy and I will talk. First I call Cathy. "The Blades want Delaney to play for them." Her response: "The same Delaney that two years ago no AAA team was interested in? Unbelievable." We agree that yes, she should play for the Blades, and Delaney thinks so too, with an emphatic "Yes" that contains zero hesitation.

And so in the fall of 2008, Delaney becomes a member of the Blades, arguably the best U16 AAA team in North America. They are the fifth different AAA team she has played for in five years, each of the previous for a step upward. But skating for the Blades is a leap upward. They will produce three All Americans for the University of Minnesota; two Harvard players who will face Minnesota for the NCAA national championship several years in the future; two future Gold Medal Olympians; and multiple other D1 college players.

The Blades play in a fall league that includes the top high school teams in the metro area: Edina, Centennial, White Bear Lake. They score eight to 10 goals per game; their opponents seldom score even one goal. In late October the Blades play in the Shattuck-St Mary's U16 tournament, and win their bracket with ease. Delaney has never skated with players who are so offensively skilled and talented: Hannah Brandt, Dani Cameranesi, Rachel Ramsey, Sami Reber, Hillary Crowe, Sam Hansen, Jonna Curtis, Kayla Mork. Delaney, Cathy and I drive the 47 miles each way to the tournament games in Fairbault. The song "Let It Rock" by Kevin Rudolph and Lil Wayne plays on the radio so frequently as we go back and forth that it becomes a musical touchstone for that week. Years later when it plays, we are back with the Blades at Shattuck in October 2008.

This is not the first time Delaney has adopted a song to listen to on the way to and from the rink while I drive her, a song that, when heard years later, evokes memories of that time and place.

During seventh grade, her initial season for St. Paul United, the song is "Closing Time" by Seismonic.

During her eighth-grade season, the song is "In a Big Country" by Big Country.

Ninth-grade season, when she is 14, it's "You Get What You Give" by the New Radicals.

As a 15-year-old 10th grader, "Into the Ocean" by Blue October.

"Hungry Like the Wolf," the old Duran Duran song, is the theme for 11th and 12th grade

But the overriding theme in her hockey career that comes from a song lyric is one we heard when "Summer of '69" played on the radio. It encapsulated her entire existence, living with the diagnosis of long QT / sudden death syndrome and the physical impact the beta blockers had on her, as well as the emotional impact implicit in all of that. I cannot quote the lyric here to avoid the risk of copyright violation. But it points to the idea that Delaney should never feel sorry for herself, and even though she had every right to make excuses, that she should not do so. The words emphasize that you should never complain when faced with adversity, but instead do what's necessary to get the job done.

VII. Better Than You

Chapter 30

In early November, as the 2008-09 St. Paul United season begins, Delaney knows that she should not talk about the hockey success she has had since the previous season ended nine months earlier. She doesn't want to be seen as boasting or bragging.

Even so, it comes as a surprise to us when at the preseason meeting the head coach holds for players and parents to discuss tryouts and the upcoming season, he makes no mention of Delaney being chosen for USA Hockey National Camp, but he does congratulate a United senior from Visitation for being a member of their state champion swim team that fall. Our perplexity increases when in the first several weeks of the season the United defense coach spends a great deal of time finding fault with everything that Delaney does on the ice, including telling her "I thought you learned something at that little camp you went to this summer." That "little camp" is not how most hockey people would describe USA national camp.

I am at the arena early one evening to pick Delaney up from practice when I see the defense coach aggressively telling Delaney that she is skating backward all wrong, that she does too many crossovers and needs to change her entire technique. Delaney not only disagrees, she does not understand why this is happening—she'd thought her coaches would be pleased at what she has accomplished and how she improved, instead of aggressively trying to bring her down. That night I call the head coach and we discuss the matter. I explain that Delaney has been taught to skate the way she does by professional instructors and that at national camp the coaches complimented her skating, both forward and backward. I ask—no, I tell him—that the defense coach should back off. We don't want her trying to alter how Delaney skates. He assures me he will put a stop to it.

In 2012 Kim McCullough, a former Dartmouth women's varsity player and founder of the company Total Female Hockey, wrote an article, "The Five-Player Rule in Hockey," about the frustration highly motivated players can experience if the bulk of their teammates lack the same drive to achieve. McCullough notes that on every team there are usually five players who are driven to get to the next level. Some people won't understand why the players are so driven, and, she writes, "some players are going to think that you think you are better than them because you are so focused and committed." On St. Paul United, it's more like the One-Player Rule, and that one player is Delaney. But her issue is not with her teammates; it's with her coaches. While McCullough discusses the challenge for coaches to help highly motivated players reach their dreams while not requiring more commitment from less motivated players, she does not address the frustration a driven player experiences when it is the coach who is the problem.

The season begins, and Delaney is playing at a high level. She will ultimately set a United record for defense scoring with 12 goals and 12 assists. She also begins drawing an average of two penalties per game from the other team when she carries the puck. Delaney also plays at the physical level that AAA hockey requires, so she accumulates her own share of penalties.

In late January 2009, at Delaney's request, we contact Shattuck about the possibility of Delaney attending school and playing hockey there the next year. They know who she is and invite her to the school to skate with the team and attend class for a day. The practice is at 7 o'clock on a minus-15-degree morning, and Delaney and I leave our house in Minneapolis at 5:30 for the drive to Fairbault. She is welcomed by the Shattuck coaches and players. The practice is high skill and high tempo, far higher than anything Delaney has experienced with United. Afterward, before classes begin, the Shattuck coach brings Delaney into the now empty dressing room and says to her: "Look around at these stalls. If you come to Shattuck, you will be surrounded by girls just like you, highly skilled and highly motivated, not just at hockey but also at school. They will be playing D1 college hockey." He then asks Delaney, "When you're in the locker room with your United teammates, is that your experience?"

Shattuck offers Delaney a place at the school and on the hockey team for the coming year. By April we have not yet decided about Shattuck—but neither have we signed a contract for the coming year with St. Paul Academy. (Though we have for Ian.) The SPA head of school, Bryn Roberts, meets with me to ask why. He also meets with Delaney, who explains her frustration with the United coaches and what she terms a culture of mediocrity.

In response Roberts arranges a meeting in his office with Delaney, Cathy and me, along with the SPA athletic director and the United head coach. When it convenes he asks Delaney to begin. She expresses her feelings with an analogy. What if United were a Spanish class? What if she was very good at Spanish and worked very hard to be so, but the class is taught for beginners, with field trips and class fiestas, and nobody improves at actually speaking Spanish ... while she is ignored, her drive and ability disregarded, and is in essence told to go sit in the corner?

At the meeting Roberts makes two decisions. First, that the "little camp" defense coach will not be with United the next season. Second, that SPA will pay for the head coach to attend a workshop on how to coach and interact with players of all levels of ability and commitment.

But Delaney must still decide. Cathy and I tell her that as a hockey player she should go to Shattuck, but that her remaining high school experience should be about much more than hockey. She is excelling at SPA and has many friends there; the school is making her a complete person. If she chooses Shattuck, she will leave all that behind, and the school dances, the prom, the softball team. Just as important, she will no longer be living at home with us. As much as we are proud of her for how good she has become at hockey we want her home with us, at least until she starts college.

Delaney finally decides: she will stay at SPA. It is the right decision. Several days later she brings home a chocolate cake, given to her at lunchtime by a senior who is captain of the football, hockey and baseball teams. Written in white frosting on top of the cake is a single word:

PROM?

Chapter 31

In April 2009 the Shattuck U19 girls' team is preparing to compete in USA Hockey's National U19 Tier One AAA championship in Boston. Their opponents will include Massachusetts Assabet Valley, Connecticut Polar Bears, Chicago Mission, Little Caesars and Belle Tire from Michigan as well as teams from Colorado, Alaska and New Jersey. Shattuck wants to play the toughest competition they can find before they leave. They ask the U16 Blades to come down and face them. The Blades may be U16, but their relative youth is irrelevant on the hockey rink.

Shattuck wins the game, but only by 4-3. They then go on to take the U19 AAA national championships, winning all their games, but with none as close as their game against the U16 Blades.

The Blades then begin play in the Two Nations Cup, a league competition in the Twin Cities and Winnipeg. Eleven U19 teams and the U16 Blades are competing, nine containing the best players in Minnesota and three teams of the best from Manitoba. The teams play a fourteen-game schedule, with contests on both sides of the border.

The top team in the regular season is from Manitoba. They lose only once, 7-6, but that loss is in Winnipeg to the Blades. The Blades finish third in league play, just behind their Minnesota archrivals, the Ice Cats.

On playoff weekend, June 5-7, 2009, the league champion Manitoba team, in the opposite bracket from the Blades, is upset in the quarterfinals. This opens the door to the championship game for the Ice Cats. Meanwhile, the Blades have no trouble advancing through their quarterfinal and semifinal.

In the Two Nations Cup grand finale, the Ice Cats lead, 2-1, as the clock ticks down. But with only a minute left, a slap shot by Rachel

Ramsey ties it for the Blades. The game goes into overtime ... but it doesn't last long. Just two minutes in, a centering pass from the left boards goes to a Blades forward in front of the Ice Cats net. She shoots it past the Ice Cat goalie and into the net. The U16 Blades have won the U19 Two Nations Cup.

For Delaney it is her first top-tier championship playing hockey. There were no titles with Washburn youth hockey nor with any previous AAA teams. United did win a Tier 3 high school holiday tournament two different years, the Sertoma Shootout, but it is a far more intense and dazzling feeling of achievement to play on a championship team at the very highest level.

Chapter 32

Delaney's improbable, almost inconceivable, ascent as a hockey player hits a speed bump in the spring of 2009. She makes the Minnesota U16 "Final 54" weekend, from which the top six defenders will be chosen and sent to the U16 national camp. But this time she is not selected. While her defensive play continues at a high level, her offensive presence does not sufficiently impress the evaluators.

As we drive home from the last Final 54 U16 competition, Delaney already senses that she will not be one of the six defense players selected for national camp. She is distressed, bordering on devastated.

It is increasingly clear that as she and her hockey peers physically mature and the tempo of play increases, she is beginning to face head-on the physical and mental limitations that come from the daily beta blockers. She gets tired more quickly and easily than the other high-level players. This limits her ability to contribute offensively and causes her to make mistakes on defense.

I don't know if Delaney recognizes this, and I don't discuss it with her, but she isn't looking for explanations or excuses—that's not who she is. Instead I see in her a heightened resolve to overcome, to succeed, to achieve her dreams.

Still, the limitations caused by the beta blockers will continue. I see no solution to this problem.

Chapter 33

In the summer of 2009 Delaney embarks on another overseas hockey adventure. In July she and Cathy depart Minneapolis for Sweden and the SwISH hockey camp ("SwISH" stands for Swedish International School of Hockey) in the southern coastal city of Landskrona. The 10-day camp is run by Sweden Women's Olympic coach Peter Elander. In a couple of years Elander will become an assistant coach for the University of North Dakota women's team, for whom he recruits European players from his SwISH camp. Most of the players are from Sweden, but there are also players from Norway, Denmark, Switzerland, Italy, Hungary and even Taiwan. They range in age from 15 to 20. Many of the names will appear on the rosters of future Swedish, Danish and Norwegian national teams and on Swedish elite league clubs. Two of the camp instructors, Pernilla Winberg and Jenni Asserholt, are already Olympic veterans skating for Sweden. There is only one attendee from across the Atlantic, and that is Delaney.

Delaney stays in a school dormitory with all the other girls, multiple beds in each room. They are on the ice three times a day—morning, afternoon and evening—but that does not mean the girls are too tired to form solid friendships. The song "Hey There Delilah" came out three years earlier, but in Landskrona the European girls reshape it into the anthem "Hey There Delaney." The hockey at the SwISH camp is something that Delaney shares in common with the other girls, but in many ways it is less meaningful than the experience and personal growth that comes from living and interacting with a group where you are the one from somewhere else. Hockey opened international doors for Delaney and her United teammates in previous summers, and at Landskrona it continues to do so for Delaney

During the camp Cathy stays in a hotel close by; Ian and I arrive with a couple days left. Then the four of us finish the adventure together by spending three days in Barcelona and four days in Mallorca. No hockey for Delaney to play in either location, and that is fine.

Chapter 34

Championship No. 2 comes in mid-August 2009; Delaney wins it at the Beantown Cup—in Boston, of course. Cathy and I planned the trip both for hockey and to go see some of the East Coast , but only I am able to go with Delaney. She is the only Midwestern player competing in the tournament; all the others on the eight competing teams are from the Northeast. The tourney is meant to expose players to Eastern colleges, and a number of D3 coaches are present. Delaney is randomly assigned to the team with the sky-blue jerseys. They win all four of their games, and she is not on ice for a single goal against.

Once the Beantown is completed we drive over the Green Mountains towards Vergennes, Vermont, stopping to see Middlebury and Coach Bill Mandigo on the way. Vergennes is the birthplace of Delaney's great grandfather, William Middlebrook, who became the vice president of the University of Minnesota. He left the family farm in 1908, and in the subsequent 100 years neither he nor any of his descendants had ever been back. Delaney and I find the farm out in the country, on Middlebrook Road no less. It wasn't a feeling like going home again, but it did feel like stepping back in time. It occurred to us on the drive back to Boston that if William Middlebrook were someplace where he was able to know where we'd been, he'd be immensely pleased.

On the drive back to Boston I also told Delaney about her great grandfather Phillip Canfield. He grew up in Wahpeton, North Dakota. The first time he ever left home was when he joined the Marines to fight in World War I. In the nightmare trenches of the Western Front he fought against the German army. He did so with such gallantry and bravery that the French government awarded him the Croix de Guerre, literally the "War Cross." He was a warrior. Delaney most definitely came from his blood.

During the Beantown Cup someone posts a poem on the notice wall at one of the rinks. No author is listed, nor can one be found after extensive search. The poem is titled "Better Than You." Its words make a powerful impact on Delaney, so much so that she writes them down on a sheet of paper to bring home with her.

Better Than You

You're better than me now
but wait awhile

You say that I am doing it wrong
but wait awhile

You laugh at me and make jokes
but wait awhile

Because while you sit there and say things
I am working harder to become better

And when I am better
I will be better than you
Just wait awhile

Delaney knows that there is no one laughing at her and making jokes. But she is very much aware that she is dealing with a tremendous physical and emotional challenge and has a much steeper mountain to climb than her hockey peers. "Better Than You" resonates deeply within her.

VIII. Why Should Hockey Be Any Different?

VIII. Why Should Hockey Be Any Different?

Chapter 35

The Upper Midwest Girls High School Elite Hockey League was formed by women's hockey icon Winny Brodt. The word "elite" is used because only the top girls' high school players are selected to play. Winny puts together three teams, colorfully named Red, Black and White, each with 15 skaters—six defense, nine forwards—and two goalies. The three elite teams play one another and the other teams in the league: the Shattuck U19 and U16 sides; the top AAA teams Belle Tire and Little Caesars from Michigan, Chicago Mission from Illinois, plus all-star teams from Wisconsin. Each team plays a total of 16 games, all on weekends from mid-September to late October so as to limit conflict with fall high school sports. Minnesota players who have attended the USA National Camp that summer are automatic invitees for Red, Black and White. The other players must try out.

Delaney is one of these other players. When the tryouts are completed she is told that she has made the cut and will be skating on the Red team, competing against the top high school and U19 players in the Upper Midwest league that fall of 2009, her junior year of high school. This is another first for a female Minneapolis-bred skater and a St. Paul United player. And it goes well—the Red team finishes at 11–5 with Delaney playing strong defense and even contributing a couple of goals.

In early November, St. Paul United are on the ice again. During the almost nine months since United's last contest Delaney has played over 50 games against high-level competition in the Elite League, the Two Nations Cup, the Beantown, the U16 final 54, as well as skating with and against the top Scandinavian players her age at the SwISH Camp in Landskrona and at Winny Brodt's summertime OS program. Only a few of her United teammates have skated at all during the interim.

For the previous couple of seasons Delaney struggled with the transition from high-skill-level, high-intensity games and practices, always with high expectations and demands, to United's practices set many bars lower. She is now a United team captain and has arranged that the team's pre-tryout captain's practices be run by Winny Brodt. It is her hope that Winny will expose the United skaters to a practice tempo and intensity they are unfamiliar with. Winny does, and the players respond enthusiastically. This is a how a practice can go? They had no idea.

As captain she asks the coach if he could increase the tempo and demands of team practices. "Why do something if you're not trying to get better at it?" she asks. "Why not strive to be the best we can be? We're expected to do this in the classrooms at St. Paul Academy and Visitation. Why should hockey be any different?"

Delaney's requests are not dismissed outright, but the coach makes no changes in his practices or his expectations. The team responds with another .500 season and another early exit from the section playoffs. Gone, again, are any aspirations for the state tournament.

Delaney finishes the season with 8 goals and 15 assists and continues to draw two opponent penalties per game. At season's end the Minnesota high school hockey coaches name her All-State Honorable Mention. She is proud of this accomplishment, but she vows that in her senior season she will be one of the six defenders in all of Minnesota to be named All-State.

Chapter 36

Delaney, Cathy and I see Dr. Ackerman again at the Mayo Clinic on November 29, 2009. Delaney, with pride, tells him about her hockey. Dr. Ackerman appears genuinely pleased for her; his ongoing support is uplifting for all of us.

She tells him she has been receiving recruitment letters from various colleges. He smiles and says we will cross that bridge when we come to it. There are no college hockey players he is aware of who have the long QT diagnosis. He notes that she is now a junior in high school who continues to be perfect in her compliance with the beta blocker therapy and remains entirely asymptomatic. Her peak heartbeat remains at less than two-thirds of her peers during stress testing.

Dr. Ackerman understands that Delaney's diagnosis is known only to the four of us in the room, as well as Delaney's brother, Ian; and her grandparents Dr. John and Phyllis Middlebrook — seven people in all. We again discuss the long QT guidelines that Dr. Ackerman has authored which prohibit Delaney from taking part in varsity hockey and softball, but by now it seems even Dr. Ackerman does not believe in these prohibitions. Delaney and the life she has lived since her diagnosis have changed his mind.

Chapter 37

Cathy and I are not the only ones who are thrilled watching Delaney skate for United and Ian for St. Paul Academy. John and Phyllis Middlebrook attend every game they can. During the 2009-10 season they are 83 and 82 years old, respectively, and their grandkids' games are the highlight of their winter. Each game, no matter how cold or inclement the weather, is an event that gets them out of the house. Before heading for the rink, they go out for dinner. They then arrive at Drake Arena early to watch the warmups and talk with the other United parents, who after four years have become their good friends.

John has Parkinson's disease and is slowly declining. He told me in his clinical doctor's voice that he now knows what he will die from, if something else doesn't get him first. Grandma Phyllis has lost most of her mobility, but with heavy reliance on a cane she is still able to slowly make her way into the arena and to her seat in the front row, where I hand her a box of popcorn and a cup of Drake Arena coffee. Grandma Phyllis can claim responsibility for the installation of the netting along the spectator side of Drake; during one game a puck flew out of the rink and missed striking her in the temple by mere inches.

It is clear to me that the joy of watching their grandchildren compete is helping keep my parents alive. John was even able to attend an away game during Delaney's sophomore season, when at the invitation of the SPA boys' junior varsity coach, she skated one game for boys' JV—the only time in her hockey career she wore the logo of her school on her chest. She played center in the game and the coach put the two biggest boys on her wings. There were no issues with the opposing team; they had no problem skating against a girl and made no attempts to physically focus on her. But apparently the SPA coach didn't tell the athletic director that Delaney would be playing. I watched as he walked into the arena, saw Delaney on the ice, then quickly left, perhaps so that he could later claim that he didn't see what he saw. The SPA team photographer, the mother of one of the boys on the team, entranced by the idea that a girl was skating with the boys, took many photos of Delaney that day. When she put together the slideshow for the boys' hockey banquet, there were at least five photos of Delaney skating in her SPA uniform.

Dr. John did miss one of Delaney's games in 2008-09, the first round of the sectional playoffs. He was having heart problems and underwent surgery. After the game Delaney, Ian, Cathy and I go directly to the hospital to see him. He is lying in a darkened recovery room, heavily medicated, half awake. Delaney carefully gives him a hug and tells him that United won the game and that she scored. He musters enough energy to give her a thumbs-up with his left hand. Without opening his eyes a smile of contentedness appears on his face.

IX. Persistence

Chapter 38

In the spring of 2010 Delaney once again earns a spot in the Minnesota Final 54 tryouts, this time at the U17 age group. But once again she is not among the six defense players selected for the USA National Camp.

The Blades, whom Delaney played for in the previous off season, have disbanded. Only two Minnesota teams will go to the NAHA tournament in Burlington, Vermont, over Labor Day, the Whitecaps and the Ice Cats. Many of the ex-Blades will join the Whitecaps, but the Ice Cats ask Delaney to skate for them. She agrees, and will play on her sixth different AAA team in as many off seasons. She does not consider this a step up or a step down; the Ice Cats are a very good team, and many of their players have already committed to D1 programs.

Before the NAHA tournament, the Ice Cats are set to compete in the Chowder Cup in Boston in early August. They hold weekly practices, run by former North Star Tom Hirsch and Bob Kuehl, the head coach of Mound Westonka High School, both of whose daughters skate for the Ice Cats. The team is managed by Tom Press and he does so as if the girls are professionals.

In the first Chowder Cup game the Ice Cats face Salve Regina, a D3 college team from Rhode Island. The tournament games are played in two halves, and after the first half of their opener the Ice Cats are leading 11-0. They go on to win 17-0, emphasizing the massive gap between top-level Minnesota high school girls' teams and a mid-level D3 college team.

After the Ice Cats win their second game by a comfortable margin they head to a quarterfinal matchup against another team made up of college players, primarily from Harvard. The final score is 2-1 for the college girls, in overtime. If a loss can be described as impressive, this was it.

Delaney, however, does not make the impression or impact that she was hoping to at the Chowder Cup. The Clarkson coach, who has been in communication with her for a couple of months, attends a game ... but alas, he says she is not what he is looking for. Other coaches provide feedback, and none of them mention Delaney's small stature, her skating ability or her defensive play. Instead the critiques focus on her apparent lack of endurance—she is not involved enough in the offense, and when she gets tired she makes mistakes. She could get by despite the beta blocker exhaustion at the lower speed of high school hockey, or on her younger off-season teams. But against the best U19 and college players she can't overcome the fatigue. The coaches don't know why Delaney lacks endurance, and she's in no position to tell them the reason. She can only vow to do better at NAHA, but she is facing a hurdle that neither willpower nor determination alone can overcome.

Delaney has persevered since she was 10. Now she has discovered an additional written motivation, just as powerful to her as the poem "Better Than You." She finds the words in a short essay written almost 100 years before by Calvin Coolidge, former president of the United States:

> Nothing in this world can take the place of persistence. Talent will not; nothing is more common than unsuccessful men with talent. Genius will not; unrewarded genius is almost a proverb. Education will not; the world is full of educated derelicts. Persistence and determination alone are omnipotent. The slogan Press On! has solved and always will solve the problems of the human race.

Delaney will ultimately incorporate some of Coolidge's words into her senior speech the following spring at St. Paul Academy. In the meantime, she is determined to persevere, both on and off the ice.

Chapter 39

Prior to the NAHA Labor Day weekend Delaney completes her third summer skating for a team of high school girls in the Women's D3 College Showcase League. The league consists mainly of D3 varsity teams from Minnesota and Wisconsin. Her team, the Blue Novas, is coached by Kevin McMullen. Incredibly, the young Blue Novas tie for the regular-season title. In the playoffs they beat Wisconsin–River Falls in the semifinal and Gustavus Adolphus in the final — and so, this team of high schoolers wins the Women's College Showcase League title. The following season both River Falls and Gustavus will advance to the NCAA D3 Frozen Four while the Blue Novas players are still on their high school teams.

Labor Day weekend arrives—time for the 2010 NAHA tournament. The North American Hockey Academy is a northeastern version of Shattuck, and since 2000 it has staged both U16 and U19 tournaments. Twenty of the top AAA teams from Canada and the U.S. compete. From the States come the host team; the Massachusetts Spitfires; Assabet Valley, also from Massachusetts; the Connecticut Polar Bears; Little Caesars from Michigan; Washington Pride from D.C.; and from Minnesota, the Whitecaps and Delaney's team, the Ice Cats; from Canada, the Ottawa Jr. Senators, Edge School, Warner School, Nepean Wildcats and the Ontario Hockey Academy. The tournament is split into four brackets of five teams each.

No Minnesota team has ever won the NAHA championship. The Ice Cats and the Whitecaps begin in separate brackets.

The Ice Cats fly into Burlington on Wednesday and lose their first game, on Thursday, 3-1 to the Edge School. Their coaches respond by telling them that winning the final three games in their bracket will send them to the quarterfinals, and that they will indeed win all three games.

The girls respond: the Ice Cats defeat the Colorado Select and Nepean Wildcats. The final round-robin game, on Saturday morning, is against the undefeated Polar Bears. The Ice Cats need to win or they are out. The final score: 6-0 for the Ice Cats. The Whitecaps also win their bracket and together with the Ice Cats advance to the quarterfinals. On Saturday afternoon the Ice Cats win their quarterfinal game against the Spitfires. The Whitecaps also win their quarterfinal game. On Sunday morning, in the semifinal, the Ice Cats again face the Polar Bears and once again they shut them out, this time by 2-0.

The Ice Cats advance to the final against Little Caesars, who beat the Whitecaps 2-1 in the other semifinal. Little Caesars is also a loaded team. Their skaters, led by 5-11 center Shiann Darkangelo (one of the best hockey names ever), will go on to play for Wisconsin, Minnesota, Boston College, Quinnipiac, Colgate, Penn State and Yale. But the Ice Cats take control of the ice from the opening draw, and halfway through the game they lead, 2-0. Yet Little Caesars persist, and finally they score midway through the final period to make it 2-1. The Ice Cats tighten their checking over the last anxious minutes. When the horn sounds it is still 2-1, the Ice Cats players piling onto their goalie in ecstatic celebration. In the stands the Ice Cat parents jubilantly hug and high-five. The Ice Cats have become the first team from Minnesota to win the NAHA tournament. It's a major accomplishment, not just for the players and the team, but for all of Minnesota girls' hockey. After losing their first game they have dominated, outscoring their remaining six opponents, 18-3. Delaney has skated every third shift in all the games alongside her defense partner, Sam LaShomb, and they are on the ice for only a single goal against. This championship is the crowning achievement of Delaney's AAA hockey career, the culmination of a step-by-step, year-by-year journey through adversity to one of the highest pinnacles of girls' hockey.

That evening the Ice Cats celebrate by taking a boat cruise on Lake Champlain before flying home to Minnesota the next morning, Labor Day. Most of the players now have D1 commitments. The list of schools they will play for is impressive: Minnesota, North Dakota, St. Cloud State, Ohio State, Harvard, Connecticut, Vermont, Quinnipiac, Maine, Syracuse. Delaney, however, still has no offers from D1 schools. She is being courted by numerous top D3 schools, like Plattsburgh, Norwich, Amherst, Elmira. She tells me she is not going to give up on her dream of playing D1 college hockey. But she is feeling the anxiety.

That evening the Ice Cats celebrate by taking a boat cruise on Lake Champlain before flying home to Minnesota the next morning, Labor Day. Most of the players now have D1 commitments. The list of schools they will play for is impressive: Minnesota, North Dakota, St. Cloud State, Ohio State, Harvard, Connecticut, Vermont, Quinnipiac, Maine, Syracuse. Delaney, however, still has no offers from D1 schools. She is being courted by numerous top D3 schools, like Plattsburgh, Norwich, Amherst, Elmira. She tells me she is not going to give up on her dream of playing D1 college hockey. But she is feeling the anxiety.

That evening the Ice Cats celebrate by taking a boat cruise on Lake Champlain before flying home to Minnesota the next morning, Labor Day. Most of the players now have D1 commitments. The list of schools they will play for is impressive: Minnesota, North Dakota, St. Cloud State, Ohio State, Harvard, Connecticut, Vermont, Quinnipiac, Maine, Syracuse. Delaney, however, still has no offers from D1 schools. She is being courted by numerous top D3 schools, like Plattsburgh, Norwich, Amherst, Elmira. She tells me she is not going to give up on her dream of playing D1 college hockey. But she is feeling the anxiety.

That evening the Ice Cats celebrate by taking a boat cruise on Lake Champlain before flying home to Minnesota the next morning, Labor Day. Most of the players now have D1 commitments. The list of schools they will play for is impressive: Minnesota, North Dakota, St. Cloud State, Ohio State, Harvard, Connecticut, Vermont, Quinnipiac, Maine, Syracuse. Delaney, however, still has no offers from D1 schools. She is being courted by numerous top D3 schools, like Plattsburgh, Norwich, Amherst, Elmira. She tells me she is not going to give up on her dream of playing D1 college hockey. But she is feeling the anxiety.

That evening the Ice Cats celebrate by taking a boat cruise on Lake Champlain before flying home to Minnesota the next morning, Labor Day. Most of the players now have D1 commitments. The list of schools they will play for is impressive: Minnesota, North Dakota, St. Cloud State, Ohio State, Harvard, Connecticut, Vermont, Quinnipiac, Maine, Syracuse. Delaney, however, still has no offers from D1 schools. She is being courted by numerous top D3 schools, like Plattsburgh, Norwich, Amherst, Elmira. She tells me she is not going to give up on her dream of playing D1 college hockey. But she is feeling the anxiety.

Chapter 40

Delaney is thrilled to have won the NAHA championship, but she is also extremely depressed that she hasn't convinced a D1 program that she can play hockey at the top collegiate level. She doesn't know how she can overcome the negatives of her beta blockers. "Is there anything else I can do?" she asks me.

I have no answers, but I do call Dr. Ackerman within days of our return from Vermont and tell him what Delaney is dealing with. I ask him if there is anything new or different that can be done to help overcome her beta blocker limitations. Dr. Ackerman tells me that yes, there is a procedure, a heart ablation, that has been developed to eliminate the health threats that come from long QT syndrome— and which will also eliminate the need for beta blockers. We drive down to see Dr. Ackerman at the Mayo Clinic.

> *Although she remains completely asymptomatic with respect to her long QT syndrome, she has grown increasingly displeased with substantial beta blocker side effects.*
>
> *The fatigue is impressive to her and unacceptable.*
>
> *This has partly been most apparent through her continuation as an elite, competitive hockey player.*
>
> —Mayo Clinic records, Dr. Michael Ackerman notes, September 14, 2010

Delaney tells Dr. Ackerman that college coaches are impressed with her skills, but they have all commented that she seems to "hit the wall" with her endurance. She tells him that the fatigue is also affecting her schoolwork and her life in general. Delaney still maintains a B-plus average at St. Paul Academy, but she is struggling. It is clear to Dr. Ackerman that her struggles are both physical and emotional.

Of course Delaney and her family know the reason.

She has concluded that it is unacceptable to continue treating her asymptomatic long QT syndrome with a program that is resulting in such extensive and unacceptable side effects.

I think we have to conclude that her current treatment program is no longer acceptable.

—Mayo Clinic records, Dr. Michael Ackerman notes, September 14, 2010

Dr. Ackerman recommends the heart ablation, a prophylactic left cardiac sympathetic denervation. The procedure involves creating tiny scars that block irregular electrical signals and restore a regular heartbeat, eliminating the potential of Delaney's heart coming to an abrupt stop. If all goes well, it will allow her to go off beta blockers and remove the possibility of an "episode" on or off the ice.

He then tells Delaney of the side effects that come from this surgery. She will no longer sweat on the left side of her face and in her left hand. It will permanently leave her with a harlequin face each time she exercises; the right side of her face will flush and become red, the left side of her face will not flush, remaining a starkly contrasting white. Additional possible side effects include a permanent left eye droop and, potentially, a permanent droop to the left side of her face. Delaney is 17 and a warrior. The decision is entirely up to her, but Cathy and I know what her decision will be.

Chapter 41

On the morning of September 17 we return to the Mayo Clinic. Delaney's heart ablation surgery will be performed that afternoon. We've told SPA that she is having a "feminine" surgery. They don't ask any further questions.

The surgeon goes through the left side of Delaney's chest to reach the nerves and perform the ablation in a video-assisted procedure. There are no complications, and she is moved to the intensive care unit for overnight monitoring. The next afternoon Dr. Ackerman comes to see her and finds no postoperative complications. He tells Delaney he is pleased with the results. She is to stay on beta blockers for three weeks, gradually reducing until she is completely off them. He then releases Delaney to come home with us to Minneapolis.

Within two days she is feeling significantly better, and only eight days after the ablation surgery she is skating in the Minnesota High School Elite League for a second fall season. Delaney does not experience the side effects of a droopy left eye or face, but in her first elite game, the harlequin face makes its appearance. Her teammates are curious. Delaney says she had nerve surgery but tells them nothing more. Technically she still has the diagnosis of long QT syndrome that would, if known about, prohibit her from playing high school sports.

Several weeks later she takes her last beta blocker, and the next morning is the first time in 2,555 days that the pill is not part of her breakfast routine. In less than a week she can feel the difference. Although her max heart rate will still permanently be limited to two-thirds that of her hockey peers, she no longer has to contend daily with the constant exhaustion that beta blockers cause. She can feel the improvement on the ice and in her daily life, including school, and Cathy and I can see it too. Delaney's anxiety and depression are gone. Now she believes she has the chance to prove she can play at the D1 level.

In the Elite League Delaney plays with a new level of endurance and stamina. Skating with defense partner Lee Stecklein, a future All-American at Minnesota and Olympic Gold Medalist, enhances the overall experience as her play surges. One highlight for Delaney: wiring a slap shot just under the crossbar past Shattuck goalie Taylor Crosby, while Taylor's older brother, Sidney Crosby, is watching.

Chapter 42

Bowdoin College in Brunswick, Maine, is a D3 athletic school. The Bowdoin Polar Bears play in the New England Small College Athletic Conference (NESCAC), together with Amherst, Middlebury, Wesleyan, Williams, Colby and Trinity. It is ranked among the Top 10 of U.S. small colleges academically. Its varsity women's hockey roster is made up primarily of graduates of New England prep schools.

Bowdoin's women's hockey program is strong, but in the last three years the team has hovered at or below .500, so in 2010 the school hired a new women's hockey coach and an athletic director who both have the goal of returning the Polar Bears to national prominence. The coach invites Delaney for a visit. Delaney understands that she has no D1 offers as yet. She also understands that Bowdoin is an exceptional school. Bowdoin has requested Delaney's SPA academic transcripts in advance. When asked to send Delaney's records to Bowdoin, the SPA college counselor tells us that although Delaney has solid grades, "her ACT score does not meet the Bowdoin minimums of at least 30. She will never be accepted at Bowdoin. Perhaps she should set her sights lower." We tell her to send the transcripts anyway.

Delaney arrives at Bowdoin on a mid-October Friday morning. She meets the coach and then is shown the hockey rink, an exceptional brand-new facility that seats 2,500. Next she attends classes and meets her potential future teammates. The visit ends with another meeting with the Polar Bears coach, who tells Delaney that Bowdoin wants to become a D3 power and that she is their No. 1 recruit and key to making this happen. She further tells Delaney that she will be offered early admission if she applies, but she needs to do so before Christmas. She flies home the next morning, and that evening Bowdoin's athletic director calls Delaney on her cellphone. He tells her this is a first for him, calling a prospective athlete at home, but he wants to emphasize to her how much Bowdoin, not only the hockey team, but also the entire college, hopes that she decides attend. He also tells her she will be accepted early admission if she applies.

Delaney liked Bowdoin very much. She knows she is fortunate to be offered early admission and is honored and flattered that Bowdoin wants her as a hockey player and student. She recognizes that time is running short and she may not be offered a chance to play at a D1 school. But she doesn't want to tell Bowdoin she'll accept early admission, and then, if a D1 offer does materialize, turn around and say she isn't coming.

As the Christmas deadline approaches Delaney still has no D1 options. Now she must make a choice; commit to attending Bowdoin or continue pursuing her dream to play D1 hockey. Cathy and I leave the decision up to Delaney; she has earned the right to make her own call on this very difficult question. Neither of us are surprised when she decides to turn down Bowdoin's offer.

We learn later that three SPA students in Delaney's class applied to Bowdoin and that none of the three, all with high grade point averages and ACT scores well over 30, are accepted. The SPA college counselor who advised that Delaney not bother applying to Bowdoin has presumably learned that being a top athlete can open college doors that academics alone cannot achieve.

X. Achieving the Impossible Dream

Chapter 43

On a December 2010 evening, St. Paul United plays Cretin–Derham Hall. Cretin is a superior high school team, as the end result, a 5-2 Cretin victory, clearly demonstrates. I watch the game while standing at the end boards with the head coach of Gustavus Adolphus, who has driven the 70 miles from St. Peter to watch Delaney play.

In the first period Delaney skates through the entire Cretin team and rifles a shot over the goalie's left shoulder, just under the crossbar, into the net. In the second period Delaney does it again, only this time her shot hits the top of the goalie's left shoulder, then drops behind her into the net. The Gustavus head coach was already interested in Delaney coming to Gustavus, but now she is one of his recruiting priorities. We discuss the merits of Delaney playing for a top D3 team like Gustavus as opposed to skating at the D1 level. "At Gustavus, Delaney will play," he says. "She'll play when it matters, when the game is on the line." He calls it a far better experience than what she might have skating D1.

Gustavus's coach speaks both from knowledge and from the heart. D1 is not only much more demanding than D3 from a time and travel standpoint, it can also be a disappointment for players who are accustomed to being a star and having large amounts of ice time. Cathy and I discuss this with Delaney. She understands, but she is not deterred. She has spent the previous three-plus years skating in the off-season with and against the best U19 players in the U.S. and Canada—and she did so while battling the side effects of beta blockers. Now that she's off them she reiterates what she told me after her eighth-grade season: "I want to play D1 college hockey." Back then it was only a wish, a 13-year-old's dream. Now it is almost within her grasp.

From the many thousands of girls Delaney's age who began their hockey careers in the late 1990s and early 2000s, only a couple hundred will become freshman D1 hockey players in the 2011-12 season. Girls from Minnesota, from across the U.S. and Canada, even from Europe—they represent a very small percentage of their hockey-playing peers. By December 2010 the positions remaining on the D1 rosters are down to a very few.

But, Delaney is a new player now that she is done with beta blockers. In addition to her quickness, aggressiveness, intensity and high hockey intelligence, she now has the endurance that the medication denied her. She becomes a dominant player for United. Winny Brodt, the main promoter of Delaney since she was 12 years old, remains both her mentor and her greatest advocate. She speaks to a number of D1 coaches on Delaney's behalf, and the D1 schools begin to notice the new Delaney.

After New Year's Delaney visits D1 Union and Niagara University in New York State, and the St. Cloud State coaches come down to watch her play at Drake Arena. With the St. Cloud State coaches on hand for a game that ends in a 2-2 tie, Delaney is being slashed, tripped, hooked and body checked each time she carries the puck. She draws three penalties at first, but as the game goes on it appears the refs have decided to call no more. Delaney is on her own. She high-sticks an opponent and receives a major penalty. I am standing near the St. Cloud State coaches when this occurs; they don't know who I am. After Delaney's high sticking major I hear one say, "That confirms it for me—I want her to skate for us."

In the end, Delaney's impossible dream, first expressed when she was a 13-year-old eighth-grader, comes down to a choice between two schools: Niagara University, just north of Niagara Falls in Lewiston, New York; or St. Cloud State University, 70 miles northwest of Minneapolis.

Delaney has never walked the ordinary path, and staying in Minnesota and skating for St. Cloud State would be just that. She'd rather take the big leap and play out east. So in early February she commits to

Niagara. Delaney will wear the uniform of the Purple Eagles (purple, of course) in the 2011-12 NCAA D1 season. Niagara and D1 hockey in the Northeast will be a challenge and an adventure, another step on the path that previously took her to Sweden and Finland with St. Paul United, then to the SwISH hockey camp in Landskrona, Sweden, as the only player from North America. With Niagara she will skate alongside teammates from across the U.S. and Canada against powerful Eastern schools: Mercyhurst, Syracuse, Boston University, Vermont, Maine, Yale, Princeton and RPI.

Delaney finishes her senior season with 11 goals and 16 assists. Her final high school goal is the only one scored by United in a 3-1 loss to Totino Grace in the sectional playoffs, as she intercepts a pass outside the blue line, splits the defense and shoots the puck just inside the left post.

She finishes her United career with 34 goals and 54 assists, both team records for a defense player (That record still stands.) In her final three high school seasons, 75 games total, she also draws an astounding 162 penalties, including 3 majors, from the other team.

Delaney is voted to the Minnesota Coaches 2010-11 Class A All-State team, one of six defense players named and the first United blueliner ever to receive the honor. The other five defenders on the All-State team all played for either the state champions, the state runner-up or the state third-place team. United's final record: 10-14.

Delaney has now achieved the two nigh-impossible goals she set for herself in eighth grade: to be named All-State and to become a D1 college player. More accolades pour in. She is named the recipient of the Athena Award at St. Paul Academy, given annually to the top female student-athlete seniors at each area high school. St. Paul Academy also awards her the Spartan Cup, as the top female student-athlete at SPA. But Delaney still has one more Minnesota high school hockey triumph coming. Every spring the Minnesota Girls' Hockey Coaches Association holds a senior fest tournament. Each of the eight sections in Minnesota girls' high school hockey presents a team of all-senior players, who compete in a weekend competition against one another. In 2011 the top players from the senior fest are selected for Team Minnesota in the National High School Invitational Tournament.

Delaney is one of the six defenders selected. She scores three goals in the national tournament and is once again not on the ice for a single goal against as Team Minnesota becomes NIT champions, defeating Team Wisconsin 4-1 in the title game. For Delaney, this completes a run of championships that also include the Two Nations Cup, the Beantown Classic, the NAHA and the Women's College Showcase League.

Finally, Delaney's high school athletic career doesn't end on an ice rink, but on a softball diamond, playing left field for St. Paul Academy. The highlight, and a perfect cap to her softball career, comes against a state softball power whose pitcher will go on to a four-year D1 college career. SPA is down, 7-2, entering the final inning. Delaney has already struck out twice, and I don't anticipate her getting a third chance, as she'd be the sixth batter in the inning. But six batters later, she is standing in the batter's box with the bases loaded and two outs. The pitch comes in. She drives it into the gap between the left- and centerfielder, and the ball rolls and rolls, because there is no fence. The bases clear, and in comes Delaney too. It's an inside-the-park grand slam! ... and the first home run the pitcher has given up in her high school career. In ending the pitcher's perfect run of no home runs given up, Delaney has put a perfect exclamation point on her own high school athletic career.

Chapter 44

Delaney's graduation party takes place on Sunday afternoon, June 19, 2011.

That morning, before the party begins, the temperature is in the low 80s but Delaney is already down the hill in Pearl Park, running sprints and intervals as part of her summer training for Niagara hockey. Her party will be more than just a celebration of a St. Paul Academy athlete who earned six letters in hockey and four in softball, serving as captain of both teams; it also celebrates a four-year member of the SPA Honor Roll, a member of the varsity debate team and the Senior Class Leadership Council, a Senior Mentor and, outside of school, a three-year student at Spanish Immersion summer camp, a member of the American Legion Auxiliary and of the Riverland Council of the Girl Scouts.

What doesn't appear on her list of accomplishments is the biggest one of all: overcoming her long QT syndrome and the side effects of beta blocker therapy from fifth grade to her senior year, not to mention her decision to undergo heart surgery. But no one can know this, including Niagara University or her Purple Eagle teammates. Because even though any risk has been eliminated, she still carries the diagnosis and, with it, the presumption of prohibition from competitive sports.

Chapter 45

In late July 2011 Delaney, Cathy and I fly to Buffalo and drive up to Niagara for Delaney's freshman orientation. She will major in business administration and minor in Spanish.

Niagara University is perched atop the Niagara River gorge, on the American side, four miles downstream from Niagara Falls and 10 miles upstream from where the river enters Lake Ontario. The Niagara River is an extraordinary Caribbean blue as it flows due north at very high speed from Niagara Falls to Lake Ontario. On the river's east bank is New York State; on the west bank is the province of Ontario. A number of battles in the War of 1812 were fought between British and American forces in the area. Later, the Underground Railroad that took many fugitives from slavery to freedom in Canada ran through towns all up and down the river, including Lewiston, home to Niagara University.

The university, founded in 1856 by the Vincentian Order, is home to 4,000 students. Niagara has presented women's D1 varsity hockey team since 1998-99. In 2002 the Purple Eagles women reached the NCAA Frozen Four but lost to Minnesota-Duluth, 3-2 in the semifinal. In the 2011-12 season they play in the College Hockey America conference, a four-team league that also includes Syracuse; Robert Morris of Pittsburgh; and national power Mercyhurst, of Erie, Pennsylvania. The '11-12 recruiting class, in addition to Delaney, consists of five other skaters: four from Canada and one from Minnesota—Kalli Funk, who played for Cretin-Derham Hall. She and Delaney will be roommates. The upperclasswomen are primarily a mix of Canadian and Northeastern players, with two skaters from Minnesota and one from Colorado. One of the captains, from Thunder Bay, Ontario, is the sister of Robert Bortuzzo, who will make his NHL debut with the Pittsburgh Penguins that same season.

During orientation the three of us explore the surrounding area, which is exceptionally beautiful. The Canadian side of the river consists of numerous orchards of apple, peach, cherry and plum trees as well as extensive and renowned vineyards. We are told that the fruit trees and grapevines on the Ontario side thrive in the microclimate created by their unique position between Lakes Erie and Ontario. Of course, we also visit Niagara Falls, which can best be described as awesome, even stunning. Delaney is beyond pleased with the school, its campus, the hockey rink, the entire area. She is excited at the prospect of spending her next four years there.

Delaney spends the entire summer of 2011 training with Winny Brodt and her OS program, skating in the summer D1 college league in Minnesota and running sprints and extensive shuttle-run sessions on her own at Pearl Park. All this training is partly due to Delaney's concern over the final element of Niagara's fall off-ice regimen, which the senior captain from Minnesota told her about: the three-minute timed shuttle run that each player must complete within a set time. Even though Delaney no longer has to contend with the fatigue from beta blockers, her max heart rate is still limited to two-thirds that of her peers.

I introduce Delaney to the 16th Street hill, not far from our house in south Minneapolis—70 yards long and rising at an incline of more than 40 degrees. Running it 10 straight times is an extreme physical challenge. Initially Delaney vomits as she runs the hill, but she persists. A couple of people whose houses face the street come out to watch as she sprints up the hill, then jogs back down to sprint up it again.

By the end of the summer Delaney can run the 10 sprints at high tempo, without losing her lunch.

Chapter 46

Delaney conquers the Niagara shuttle-run minimum required time with one second to spare, her harlequin face at its finest—bright red on the right side, white as a pearl on the left. The ice training then begins. Niagara has seven defenders competing for ice time. The first two exhibition games, in late September, are against Canadian U19 teams. I fly to Buffalo and drive a rental to Niagara to watch Delaney play. She wears No. 2, and this is the first time, for all the teams that she skated for, that I've seen her wearing purple. She plays extremely well. I fly home confident that she will get solid ice time during the season.

The Purple Eagles open their 2011-12 season with a two-game set against New Hampshire at Dwyer Arena on the Niagara campus. With the help of our friends the Knutsons, Cathy and I find the livestream and transfer it to their big-screen TV. There is no sound, but we see that it is Delaney who scores Niagara's first goal of the season, and in her college D1 debut. She crashed the net and stuffed in a rebound. We can't tell if the puck goes in off her stick or off her body, but that doesn't matter; the goal counts. Niagara winds up losing both games to New Hampshire, 6-3 and 3-2, but Delaney is not on the ice for a single goal-against and goes plus-2 for the series. The CHA names her Rookie of the Week.

Cathy and I travel east to watch Delaney and Niagara in person as much as we can. At home we watch every game via livestream on our computer, including a two-game sweep of RPI, where in the first game Delaney plays a pivotal role. Niagara is losing, 4-3, with two minutes remaining when an RPI skater pulls down Delaney in the neutral zone. On the ensuing power play the Purple Eagles score to tie it up, setting the table for the OT winner.

On December 2 Cathy and I fly to Columbus for a two-game series at Ohio State. Ian comes with us. Our joy at watching Delaney play in person is magnified when we see how proud he is of his sister. In February I even watch the Niagara livestream from 10 time zones away, in Almaty, Kazakhstan, where I am head coach of the U.S. National Team competing in the Men's Bandy World Championship. The Purple Eagles are playing Mercyhurst at Erie, Pennsylvania, but no problem. I wake up in the middle of the night to watch the game.

The 2011-12 Niagara season ends with the Purple Eagles at 10-16-8. Delaney has had a very good year, both on and off the rink. On the ice she has proven herself to be a legitimate D1 defense player. Off the ice she has made solid friends, among both her teammates and classmates. Her grades are excellent, and she is named to the CHA All-Academic team. An off-ice highlight for Delaney is the volunteer service work that Niagara requires of all the players on the women's hockey team. Delaney is introduced to a teenage boy with multiple physical and mental challenges. She becomes a big sister to him. One of his favorite activities with her is when they go skating together on rinks at Niagara and in Buffalo. She even gets to meet Willie O'Ree, who in 1958 became the first Black player in the NHL.

She is excited about her next three years at Niagara. It is the perfect school and the perfect hockey team for her.

XI. The Nightmare

Chapter 47

During spring break, in early March, after Niagara's season has ended, Delaney and several of her teammates go to Cancun for a week: a vacation from the demands of five months of school and six months of hockey. Two weeks later Cathy and I are also on vacation, with our friends the Knutsons, in Aruba, just off the coast of Venezuela. One day into the vacation, on a hot, bright sunny day, Scott Knutson and I are sitting by the pool at the hotel bar. My cellphone rings. It's Delaney, with something extremely upsetting to tell me—so much so that she can hardly get it out between sobs.

The Niagara coach has just met with the team. He has informed them that Niagara University has decided to drop the women's varsity hockey program. There will be no Niagara women's team the following season. The players can choose to remain at Niagara, and their scholarships will be honored, but they will not be playing hockey for the Purple Eagles.

Cathy and I know that Delaney is absolutely devastated by this announcement. We both feel as if we have been hit very hard in the stomach and all the air has been knocked out of us. We want to fly home to Minnesota and try to help Delaney figure out what she will do for school and hockey the following year. We have six days remaining, however, in the now not-so-paradisiacal Aruba.

The timing of Niagara's announcement could only have been worse if it occurred just before the next school year started. It's still very bad. Almost all D1 women's hockey teams have completed their recruiting in early March, both in terms of available scholarship money and in filling roster positions. The Niagara players begin the scramble to find another school. Some upperclass players will choose to remain at Niagara and complete their educations. Some will attend a different school the following season but will not play hockey. And some will find schools and D1 programs to transfer to.

Three players end up at Mercyhurst, where they will form a line as the Lakers advance to the NCAA women's Frozen Four. Others will end up at Robert Morris, Syracuse, St. Lawrence, Lindenwood and St. Cloud State. The week after Niagara's announcement Delaney is inundated with emails from Eastern D3 schools, perennial national contenders and aspiring programs alike: Bowdoin, Amherst, Trinity, Norwich and Plattsburgh State. In the Midwest Gustavus and St. Scholastica are the premier D3 schools that court her. Ultimately, coaches from 30 different schools contact her. She shares each email with me in Aruba. Delaney responds politely to each coach. With some she leaves the door open, and with others she simply thanks them for their interest.

Cathy and I return to Minneapolis, and Delaney comes home from Niagara for Easter weekend. On Saturday morning, April 7, Delaney and I are driving to the grocery store when her cellphone rings. It's the head coach of the women's varsity at D1 Rensselaer Polytechnic Institute calling. He saw Delaney play for Niagara in their two games against RPI the previous October. He tells Delaney that he'd like her to attend RPI the following year and skate for the Engineers. First, she needs to come for a visit to meet the players to confirm that they like Delaney and that Delaney likes them.

The weekend after she returns to Niagara for the spring semester Delaney takes the six-hour train ride from Buffalo to Troy, New York, where RPI is located. She spends the weekend with the RPI players and makes a good impression. The coach formally offers Delaney a position on his team for the 2012-13 season—contingent, of course, on her being accepted as a student.

RPI, founded in 1824, is primarily an engineering university, but it also has a strong business program. It is an excellent school with an excellent academic reputation. Located in the hills above the Hudson River, the campus is majestic. RPI women's hockey plays in the Eastern College Athletic Conference, together with the Ivies (Harvard,

Yale, Princeton, Dartmouth, Cornell and Brown), Clarkson, Quinnipiac, St. Lawrence, Colgate and Union. Delaney's grades at Niagara in her business administration classes are excellent, which helps her get accepted at RPI. There is only one requirement before Delaney can begin classes in the fall of 2012: she must take and pass a calculus class, mandatory for all incoming students.

In summer school at the University of Minnesota, Delaney conquers calculus. In August 2012 she begins her RPI career as a sophomore student and varsity hockey player for the Engineers.

Chapter 48

During the summer of 2012 Delaney prepares for the upcoming RPI hockey season just as she prepared for her initial college season at Niagara. She trains with Winny Brodt and the OS program and skates in the women's D1 college league. Even though RPI does not have a timed shuttle run that she must conquer, she continues to run the sprints and intervals at Pearl Park together with attacking the formidable 16th Street hill. The same neighbors who came out to watch the previous summer come out again to see her run the 10 sprints in 80-plus-degree heat. Delaney is joined by her former Ice Cat teammate Greer, who plays for Vermont. (Cathy also runs the hill, as a show of support but also as a mental stress reliever at the end of a long day in the office. She also vomits during the workout.) The only addition to Delaney's summer is the calculus class at the University of Minnesota. In late August Cathy and I fly with Delaney to Albany, then make the short drive to Troy and RPI to help her move into her dorm.

The RPI Engineers play their home games at the Houston Field House, an on-campus rink that opened in 1949 but has since undergone major renovations. Seating 4,780, it features a large, modern four-sided electronic scoreboard the equal of any in college hockey. RPI has twice won the NCAA men's national championship, and many players have gone on to play in the NHL.

The RPI women's hockey program first competed as a D1 NCAA team in the 2005-06 season. Their dressing room is large and professional, carpeted, with the RPI logo in the center of the floor. Long-standing hockey tradition states that stepping on the logo is bad luck. I am quickly informed of this when I accidentally place my foot on it. I remove my foot, hoping I haven't offended the hockey gods and caused potential misfortune for Delaney.

The team roster has more American players on it than Niagara, but it still contains a number of Canadians. Many of the RPI players come from the Northeast, but there are a few Midwesterners, including three in addition to Delaney from Minnesota, and even two from Alaska. For the 2012-13 season the Engineers will have seven defense on the roster; the previous season the team suffered numerous injuries to its defense players, and Delaney has been brought in as insurance.

When the season begins, one of the defense, a senior captain from Ontario, is still recovering and Delaney takes a regular shift and plays very well. When that player returns several weeks later, RPI still dresses seven defenders for each game, but the coach also plays Delaney at forward.

However, she is not on the penalty kill, so she meets with the head coach to tell him she is good at it, and that she was a regular on Niagara's penalty kill. She asks him to give her a chance to prove herself. The coach responds that RPI's defense is better than Niagara's was and declines her request. Delaney does not bring up the fact that Niagara beat RPI in both games the previous season, and that the Purple Eagles' penalty kill, with her on it, shut down RPI's power play. She recognizes that pointing this out would not be well received.

Although she is happy to be at RPI, Delaney is neither satisfied nor fulfilled with her first season. She returns to Minnesota, focusing on a demanding on-and-off-ice training program, again with Winny Brodt, and plays in the D1 summer college league. Her summer also involves significant weight training, something RPI emphasizes as part of their players' off-season regimen. Delaney has grown an inch and is now 5-5 and 140 pounds with the added muscle—all aimed at the goal of earning regular ice time. When she returns to RPI in August she is surprised to learn that several of her teammates, including one of the captains, have for the most part taken the summer off from skating and training, certain that this will have no impact on how much they play.

The season begins with two exhibition games against U19 teams from Canada. Cathy and I are able to watch on the computer as

Delaney's performance shows the positive impact of her summer training. She even notches two assists — double her total for the previous season.

Then Delaney's long QT syndrome is discovered. The hammer falls.

One of the off-ice trainings involves heavy sprinting while the players are wearing heart monitors to assess their endurance and recovery time. The athletic trainer running the session notes two things about Delaney. First, her harlequin face during and after the sprints. Second, that her max heart rate never crosses 130 beats per minute during the session, while the other players' heartbeats all rise to between 180 and 200. He is familiar with heart ablation surgery and its side effects. After the training session he pulls Delaney aside.

"Have you had a heart procedure?" he asks her.

Cathy and I have discussed with Delaney how she should respond if she is ever asked this question: with the truth. But we have also told her that if asked the natural follow-up, "Why didn't you tell us?," that she should respond with, "My father told me not to." We want the blame, and the repercussions, to fall on us, not Delaney.

And so she responds to the athletic trainer, "Yes, I have."

Chapter 49

The sprint training took place in the morning, before classes begin. Delaney calls me afterward, extremely upset, concerned that she will be dismissed from the hockey team. I call Cathy to tell her what has happened, that Delaney's secret, after 10 years, is no longer a secret. None of us knows what will transpire next, but I tell Cathy I will call the head coach that afternoon.

I cannot fault him for the extreme anger he directs at me, but I try to explain Delaney's situation, that her doctor at the Mayo has fully cleared her to play, and that because of the ablation surgery there are no risks to her health. He hears none of what I have to, or want to, say. Instead he tells me that Cathy and I are the worst possible parents, not only putting Delaney's health and life at risk, but also not telling him and RPI about her diagnosis. He goes on for several minutes, continuing to rip me a new one. I know better than to try to interrupt. I have to hold my cellphone away from my ear, such is the volume of his voice and the angry heat coming from through it—I'm concerned that my ear will catch fire, or even my entire head. The coach tells me that Delaney will not be allowed to practice with the team until RPI's doctor contacts Dr. Ackerman, and that Cathy and I will be required to come to Troy to meet the RPI doctor and explain ourselves and our disgusting behavior as parents. I tell him that I understand and that I, of course, agree. I then call Dr. Ackerman. When he calls me back he tells me that he has already had a long conversation with the RPI doctor.

"We knew this would happen at some point Chris," he says. "It is rather extraordinary that it took so long to come out." Dr. Ackerman tells me he has confirmed for the RPI doctor that there are no risks for Delaney to continue to train and play hockey at the D1 level. From a medical standpoint, Dr. Ackerman emphasized, she can be reinstated to the RPI hockey team immediately. The RPI doctor, however, confirms that before reinstatement can occur, Cathy and I must first come out to RPI and meet him in person. So that is what we do.

At the meeting in the doctor's office on the RPI campus, Cathy and I again are berated for keeping Delaney's diagnosis a secret, and for telling her to also keep it a secret. How to respond? We could tell the doctor what he already knows, that Delaney's specialist has confirmed that she faces no long QT health risks from playing hockey. We could tell him that despite that, if she had told the RPI coach about her diagnosis he never would have offered her a place on the team. We could have told him that playing D1 hockey probably means more to Delaney than most other D1 players, and that very few women worked harder and overcame greater adversity than Delaney did to play D1. Finally, we could have leaned forward in our chairs, looked him in the eye and told him point blank that neither he nor the coach have any idea what Delaney has lived through, and we are the best parents she could ever have.

But we don't say any of this. We recognize that the doctor won't understand. Instead, our biggest concern is that she be allowed to remain on the team, and we don't want to jeopardize that further by anything we say or do. Apparently we come across to the doctor as thoroughly chastised and contrite, because he then tells us that from a medical standpoint, Delaney will be allowed back on the team. But, he says, even though he'll approve Delaney's immediate return to hockey, Dr. Ackerman must, by January, conduct a full and complete evaluation on her again.

The RPI coach will no longer speak to me, so I send him a lengthy email explaining Delaney's entire history, that per Dr. Ackerman she did not have any health risk playing hockey for Rensselaer, and the reasons behind the actions and decisions Cathy and I took. I ask him for his understanding and forgiveness, and although I include no specific language asking for it, I also want him to show mercy toward Delaney. It is my hope that he will recognize that he has never had a player who has worked so hard and overcome so much to reach the level she has. He never responds to my email, nor does he ever once talk with Delaney about her diagnosis or all that she has done over the years to live with and overcome it. If he had spoken to her, he'd have been forced to recognize her as a person and could not treat her so heartlessly. Delaney, who has never discussed her diagnosis with anyone besides us and Dr. Ackerman, doesn't know how to talk about it with her teammates — she is alone. To help her cope with the emotional and psychological fallout, she starts counseling with the school psychologist.

Chapter 50

Delaney returns to the team the same day that Cathy and I meet with the RPI doctor, but the coach has made her an outcast. No longer is she concerned about whether she will skate on the penalty kill or how much ice time she will get. In many of the RPI games she does not even dress, instead sitting in the stands, watching the team play. In practices the coach excludes her from coordinated defense drills with a partner, while ignoring her presence on the ice. One teammate has the courage to speak up for Delaney. That player is benched for a game.

RPI is coming to Minnesota over Thanksgiving to play a two-game series against St. Cloud State. The coach is quoted in an RPI press release saying that this will be an opportunity for the five Minnesota girls on the roster to play in front of their families. It will be the first time that Delaney will play a college game in Minnesota, if the coach allows it. She knows that Cathy and I will be at both games, whether she suits up or not, but she also knows this will probably be the only chance for her now 87- and 86-year-old grandparents, Dr. John and Phyllis, ever to see her play college hockey in person. Both are now in assisted living, and it will take some planning to bring her grandmother the 75 miles to St. Cloud to see her play. Delaney knows better than to ask the head coach which game, if either, she might play, so she goes to the defense coach and asks her instead.

"I knew you would come asking this," Delaney is told. "It is selfish of you to even ask—you are thinking only of yourself and not the team." The defense coach declines to tell Delaney which, if any, game she will dress for. She will learn of the decision on game day. This makes it impossible for Cathy and I to arrange for Grandma Phyllis to see Delaney play.

One month later Grandma Phyllis falls into a coma and is given Last Rites. Although she will awaken after several weeks, she never leaves her bed again. She dies without ever having seen her "selfish" granddaughter skate as a college player.

That weekend Delaney suits up for the first game, vs. St. Cloud State, and plays eight shifts. The morning of the second game Delaney is told she will not be dressing, and although she knows this was coming she falls apart emotionally. Cathy and I immediately drive up to St. Cloud and meet Delaney at the rink. We sit in the stands with her and work to calm her down. After that game we meet with the head coach and the defense coach. Cathy reminds the coach of his quote, that playing in Minnesota will give the families of the Minnesota girls the chance to watch them play in person. Cathy then tells him that not telling Delaney which game she would play in until game day is "just cruel." She tells him that although she can understand why he would dislike her and me, she cannot understand why he would treat Delaney so badly, with such cruelty, especially when he knows all that she has overcome to be who she is as a hockey player and as a person.

"You should be ashamed of yourself," she tells the coach. He is unable to offer an explanation or an excuse and stands there looking, yes, ashamed.

He does, however, suggest that we take Delaney home with us that night so she can emotionally recover. We inform him that we have already discussed this with Delaney and she has told us she will be returning with the team to RPI. She is a member of the team, regardless of how the coach treats her.

Delaney stays with the team, rooming that night with one of the captains, Jordan, who is not only the team's best player, she is also calm and kind. But first there is a team gathering, a party at the family home of two RPI skaters, sisters, whose parents live in Coon Rapids. Perhaps ironically, considering the circumstances, Cathy and I have covered 50 percent of the food and drink cost of the party. The team will then take their bus to the hotel at the Minneapolis-St.

Paul airport. For Cathy and me, the gathering is an extraordinarily uncomfortable evening. Delaney behaves as if nothing happened that day, or since the head coach learned of her diagnosis. But when she says goodbye to us, she cries. Then Jordan walks her to the team bus, her arm around Delaney's shoulder. As they get on the bus Cathy also begins to cry, while my eyes fill with tears.

XII. The Real Hero in All This

Chapter 51

Delaney returns home to Minneapolis in mid-December for a two-week holiday break. The majority of the RPI student body has the month of January off, but not the hockey players. They will return to Troy just after New Year's. On Tuesday, December 17, 2013, Delaney, Cathy and I drive down to Rochester and the Mayo Clinic to meet with Dr. Ackerman so that updated testing can be performed as required by the RPI doctor. The tests are performed that afternoon and that night we stay at a hotel a couple of blocks from the Mayo.

The next morning we meet with Dr. Ackerman who greets Delaney as if she were his own daughter. She has been his patient since September 2003, but their relationship is much more than that. Dr. Ackerman has been an essential part of Delaney's life since she was 10 years old, watching her grow from a little girl to a teenager to a young adult, guiding, supporting and encouraging her, at the risk of his own medical reputation, through her decade-long crusade to overcome the harsh limitations imposed by her long QT syndrome diagnosis. He has helped her to live a full life, to be the athlete, the competitor, the person, that she was born to be.

As the four of us sit in his office on that December morning, I know that Dr. Ackerman celebrates Delaney's accomplishments, her successes as a hockey player and as a person. She has beaten the diagnosis of long QT syndrome. She has overcome the major limitations presented by the beta blockers. She has with absolute conviction and courage accepted both the certain and potential side effects of heart ablation surgery. And Dr. Ackerman knows it.

Delaney is an extraordinary young woman.
She endured many years of profound side effects from the beta blockers before the denervation (ablation) alternative was pursued.

She has really blazed the trail in so many ways.

Delaney has been one of my personal inspirations that gave me the confidence to challenge the long QT syndrome status quo over a decade ago. Back then her family's decision was really quite unique."

—Mayo Clinic records, Dr. Michael Ackerman notes, December 18, 2013

Dr. Ackerman tells us directly that there are now multiple athletes in different sports competing at the D1 level who would not be but for the decisions we made as a family for Delaney back in 2003, and the courage and determination that Delaney has shown ever since.

The bottom line is Delaney's parents, and Delaney herself, have been instrumental in enabling Mayo Clinic's experience with athletes with disqualifying genetic heart conditions to live and thrive despite their condition and to remain engaged in the thing that they love.

Delaney's amazing spirit refused to resign to the status quo and instead she chose to live life large despite her potentially life-threatening condition.

She should be viewed as the real hero in all this.

—Mayo Clinic records, Dr. Michael Ackerman notes, December 18, 2013

Cathy and I already knew that what Delaney has overcome and accomplished is almost inconceivable. But we had never considered the impact Delaney had on the decision-making of Dr. Ackerman and other long QT experts, and thus her immense impact on the lives of other athletes with the long QT diagnosis. We are beyond proud of our daughter.

Dr. Ackerman writes a letter to RPI, for the coach and the school to read, stating what he has told us and what he has written in his notes. He too does not want to see the RPI coach continue to punish Delaney by denying her the opportunity to compete, something that long QT failed to do.

If the RPI coach ever reads the letter, he declines to acknowledge it to Dr. Ackerman, Cathy or me, or to Delaney. Instead, he keeps

shunning her during practices and not dressing her for games. When she misses a morning conditioning session because she is seeing the counselor for her mental health he punishes her with extra conditioning. She will suit up for only 20 of RPI's 33 contests in 2013-14. At the season-ending banquet there is a slideshow presentation for the players and their families, action photos of all the players. All the players, that is, except for Delaney—there are no photos of her in the slideshow. The RPI coach has apparently decided that rather than treating Delaney as the hero Dr. Ackerman describes her as, or even as a regular member of his team, he will try to demoralize her until she quits.

Chapter 52

Playing D1 college hockey and being a solid student are not mutually exclusive. Instead the two go hand in hand. I thought about this during Delaney's sophomore year at RPI, on a weekend where the Engineers played Dartmouth and Harvard on consecutive nights. Seven former girls from Blake Prep School in Minneapolis were skating for the two teams, four for Dartmouth and three for Harvard. I was certain these girls were receiving an excellent education while playing D1 hockey. RPI, academically rated very high nationally, also emphasized to its hockey players the importance of doing well in their studies. The vast majority of the players on the team had GPAs over 3.0. This included Delaney, who was named to the ECAC All-Academic team all three of her years at RPI. In fact, the majority of players on almost every single women's D1 college hockey team were solid students.

It was no surprise that after her junior season at RPI Delaney decided to not devote her summer to hockey training. She figured it wouldn't matter how prepared she was for hockey when she returned to RPI as a senior in late August, nor would it matter whether her teammates had worked hard in the summer to be better. The RPI coach had made it clear to Delaney that she would play very little.

Thus, instead of hockey in the summer of 2014, Delaney enrolled at the London School of Economics for a six-week course on negotiations. The class would satisfy credit requirements for her business administration major while she learned an important skill. In addition, she would be living in London, studying with classmates from all over Europe and the world. It was the first time since 2005, when Delaney was 12, that her off-season did not revolve around training for hockey. It was a magnificent summer.

Chapter 53

"Great moments come from great opportunities," Herb Brooks once told the 1980 U.S. Olympic hockey team. Sometimes, however, opportunity comes from the misfortune of others.

In October 2014, Delaney's senior season, RPI opens its schedule with games against the University of North Dakota in Grand Forks and Bemidji State in Bemidji. As the seventh defense player Delaney takes about eight shifts in each game, a 7-1 loss to North Dakota and a 4-0 loss to Bemidji State. She plays very well, and is not on the ice for any of the 11 combined goals the opponents score. But one of the RPI defenders, Heidi Niskanen from Finland, sustains a concussion during the Bemidji State game. It is her third diagnosed concussion, and the symptoms persist upon her return to Troy. Her season is over, and worse, so is her hockey career.

Heidi's misfortune makes Delaney the No. 6 defender. She will now dress for and play every game—but she is still treated by the coach as a spare, never taking the ice for the penalty kill, and inevitably the coach glues her to the bench near the end of the third period or if the game goes into overtime. Even though Delaney is seldom on the ice for a goal-against and has the best plus-minus mark of anyone in RPI's blueline corps, the coach has decided that she will not play when the game is on the line—even as the Engineers lose almost every one of these close games.

When the team photo is taken the coach attempts to break with the tradition that places all the seniors in the front row. He personally tries to put Delaney at the end of the upper row. But his very disturbing attempt is foiled by team captain Mari Mankey, who insists that Delaney sit in the front row with the other seniors. The coach backs down. And what can Delaney do about it? In the past, when she has encountered a bully, she has always acted quickly to shut them down. Now she is powerless, except being able to make it clear that she will endure.

The emotion that best describes how Cathy and I are feeling about Delaney's dilemma is rage. It is an impotent rage, one that has no outlet and which definitely interferes with our ability to sleep at night. We, too, are powerless, and must endure.

I am at RPI in early December 2014 to watch a home series. The second game is on Saturday afternoon. Delaney and I then have dinner and go to a movie, "Unbroken." It tells the true story of an American, Louis Zamperini, who runs track in the 1936 Olympics, but in World War II becomes a Japanese prisoner of war after his plane crashes in the South Pacific. At the prison camp he becomes the target of a cruel camp commander, known to the prisoners as "the Bird," who tries to break Zamperini but is not successful. The movie has a tremendous impact on Delaney. She tells me that the Bird is exactly who and what the RPI coach is to her. She still cannot comprehend the meanness and cruelty that he continues to show to her. She tells me the coach has not broken her yet, and that she will make sure that he never does.

Chapter 54

RPI has a home series vs. the Rochester Institute of Technology in late November 2014. They will have only four defenders in the Friday night game, as the coach has imposed a one-game suspension on a number of RPI players for unspecified disciplinary reasons. Delaney is one of the four defenders who dress for the game. She plays every other shift and is on the penalty kill for the first time since her freshman year at Niagara. The coach has no choice. RPI wins the game, 4-1. All four defense players shut down the RIT power play and have a strong game.

Watching Delaney play the full game, Cathy and I are struck by what could have been. It is not a bittersweet emotion, just bitter. The next afternoon RPI is back to six defense and Delaney is returned by the coach to her second-class role. They lose to RIT, 3-0.

The home stretch of the 2014-15 RPI hockey season runs from January 2 to February 21, a total of 17 games. RPI's record in these games is 4 wins, 12 losses, 1 tie. They score 31 goals and give up 54. Delaney is seldom on the ice when the opponent scores. She plays smart and solid, and finishes her RPI career confirming that she is a D1 hockey player. Cathy, Ian and I go out to Troy for the final two games of the season on February 20 and 21 vs. Cornell and Colgate. RPI loses 4-1 to Cornell on Friday night. The next day Cathy, Ian and I pick Delaney up at her apartment to go out for a late breakfast. This is a Saturday tradition that we have followed all four years of Delaney's college hockey career when we've been in New York State to watch her play.

On the way to the restaurant Delaney plays a CD that she made especially for this final occasion. The songs are those we listened to while going to and from the rink during the six years of Delaney's high school hockey career. They are the musical theme to so many years: "Closing Time," "You Only Get What You Give," "Let It Rock," "In a Big Country," "Into the Ocean," "Hungry Like the Wolf," and the finale, that she only listened to once in the car with me, began sobbing, and wouldn't listen to again—"Father and Daughter," by Paul Simon.

I am not prepared for the tidal wave of emotion that hits me in my face and in my heart. Seventeen years of hockey memories, a gallery of images and emotions, fills my head, one by one, until the final frame is reached: Delaney is once again 4 years old. I hold her in my arms up to the glass at Parade Ice Gardens so she can see her brother skate. Her little girl voice, crystal clear, telling me, "I promise, Dad, that I will never be a quitter."

Prior to the Saturday afternoon game vs. Colgate there's a reception for the players' parents in the VIP section of the rink. I am sitting eating a sandwich when one of the assistant coaches comes and kneels next to me. He has something to tell me, although he has some difficulty doing so. He needs to tell me without saying anything directly about the head coach. He acknowledges that Delaney is a good player and a good person and that she has received rough treatment from RPI hockey. She deserves far better than she has received, and he is sorry he couldn't make a difference.

Colgate is favored to win the final game, but RPI plays one of their best games of the season. So does Delaney, finishing her RPI career on a high note. With 45 seconds remaining, the score is 5-3 for RPI. The five senior skaters, Delaney included, are on the ice, along with the senior goaltender. Tradition dictates that the seniors finish their careers on the ice, especially if the result of the game is already decided. A whistle blows with 20 seconds left, and RPI hockey directs one final act of cruelty toward Delaney. The defense coach tries to take her off the ice. But the junior defender that has been told to take Delaney's place refuses to go on, telling Delaney, "Stay out there." She does. The game ends 5-3 for the Engineers, and Delaney finishes her RPI hockey career and her association with the head coach damaged, but unbroken.

XIII. A Hockey Pro in Sweden

Chapter 55

Delaney's collegiate hockey career is over, but she still has more than two months of classes at RPI before she gets her diploma. Delaney's hockey experience at RPI has been unfulfilling, unpleasant and at times traumatic. She has no intention of finishing her hockey journey on such an unsatisfying note. In mid-March she returns to Sweden for the first time since she attended the SwISH Hockey Camp in Landskrona in the summer of 2009. She is hoping to play for a team in the Swedish Elite League—the Riksserien, the best women's hockey league in Europe—for the 2015-16 season.

This has been an aspiration of Delaney's since her freshman year of college, strongly encouraged by Cathy and me. I played bandy professionally in Sweden for two years in the mid-'80s, and I had been to Sweden more than 30 times since to play and coach bandy, as well as for several summer vacation trips with Cathy. In addition, living in Sweden had already become a family tradition. In 2012 Ian played bandy for Skirö, a club in southern Sweden, after spending four months in Arkhangelsk, in the far north of Russia, with the Russian Super League club Vodnik.

Delaney never considered trying to play for a team in the U.S. and the newly formed National Women's Hockey League. She was well aware that after being buried at RPI she was unlikely to elicit much interest from NWHL clubs. On top of that, from a hockey standpoint alone, the NWHL was limited. There were only four teams, playing just 18 games each; the well-established Riksserien was entering its ninth season, with 10 teams playing 36 games each, plus playoffs. Even more important, Delaney understood that playing hockey in Sweden could offer life experiences far greater than whatever she'd get from playing in the United States.

The Riksserien, established in 2007 by the Swedish Ice Hockey Federation, consists of 10 teams in '15-16: Luleå, MoDo, Leksand, Sundsvall, AIK, Linköping, Brynäs, SDE, Djurgården and HV71. All teams play on Olympic-size ice sheets, from September through February, with the top eight advancing to playoffs in late February and March. Meanwhile the two bottom finishers compete in a relegation playoff with the winners of each of Sweden's four regional First Divisions (the second tier of the Swedish women's ice hockey pyramid); those six teams battle it out to determine who will fill the final two spots in the Riksserien the following season.

The players in the Riksserien are not all Swedes, not by a long shot. They come from all across the hockey-playing world: Finland, Germany, Austria, Norway, Denmark, France, Switzerland, Hungary, Italy, Russia, Latvia, Slovakia, the Czech Republic, Poland, even Spain, the Netherlands, the U.K. and Japan. It is the most international hockey league in the world. Canada, of course, is well represented in the Riksserien—but as of 2015 only a handful of Americans have played in the league, and only one played for a team that won the Swedish championship.

There are two main reasons for the dearth of Americans. The first is that Sweden is still not well known as a post-college women's hockey destination. The second is the significant immigration and visa restrictions that Sweden has placed on Americans, which make it difficult and expensive for Riksserien teams to have American players on their rosters beyond a 90-day period.

Delaney stays in Stockholm with family friends, Stefan and Anna Erixon. While there she skates with two Stockholm clubs in what are, in essence, informal tryout sessions. One, AIK, was founded in 1891; its women's hockey team beginning play in the Riksserien in 2008, where they quickly earned championships in 2009 and 2013. In the just-completed '14-15 season, AIK lost the playoff final to Linkoping. Delaney has a history of her own with AIK, having played against the club's girls' team as a member of touring St. Paul United in 2006.

Delaney also joined Djurgården for a practice at Hovet Arena, which is attached to the Globen, Stockholm's top ice arena.

Djurgården, founded in 1897, started its participation in women's hockey only in 2014, but needed just one season to move up to the Riksserien, having blown past every one of their First Division opponents. After the training session she meets with Nils Ekman, Djurgården's general manager and a former NHLer who once played on a line with Sidney Crosby. He is honest with Delaney. He tells her she has proved herself as a player, but Djurgården is looking for the highest-level player, an all-star, and that is not Delaney. He is unable to offer her a contract.

AIK, however, does. Delaney returns to RPI confident that she will play for AIK in the 2015-16 Riksserien season. ... But wait—the AIK board of directors rescinds the contract offer. They have determined that Delaney will cost the club too much money.

Now the third club playing out of Stockholm, SDE, contacts Delaney about skating for them the following season. So does another club, HV71 of Jönköping, put in touch with Delaney through Magnus Sköld, the same person who helped arrange the St. Paul United hockey trips to Europe. Like Djurgården, HV71 has just risen to the Riksserien from the First Division. Discussions begin between Delaney and HV71 and continue through April and May.

In early June 2015, on an extremely hot day in Troy, Delaney receives her Bachelor of Arts diploma from RPI, having graduated with a cumulative 3.4 GPA. For the third straight year she is named to the ECAC All-Academic team.

One week later she signs a contract to play for HV71. She is headed to Sweden for the 2015-16 Riksserien season, as a professional hockey player.

Chapter 56

Two weeks before she leaves for Sweden to begin her pro hockey career, Delaney decides to see Dr. Ackerman at the Mayo Clinic. Her visit does not involve any health concerns; those have been resolved by her heart surgery. Rather, she simply wants to connect with him again. Over the years he has become much more than just her physician. She and Dr. Ackerman are good friends.

This is her first visit in 19 months, when he lauded her as a trailblazer and hero for high school and college athletes with long QT syndrome. Now Delaney is taking it one step further. She is about to become the first professional athlete with the long QT diagnosis.

Dr. Ackerman notes that nothing has occurred since the last time he saw her that would prohibit Delaney from playing hockey in Sweden. The heart denervation surgery continues to be a complete success. Her max heart rate has also improved; it is now three-quarters that of her peers, rather than the two-thirds she competed at in high school and college.

> *I continue to be fully supportive of Delaney's pursuit of professional hockey.*
>
> *I have been supportive of her since the day I met her.*
>
> —Mayo Clinic records, Dr. Michael Ackerman notes, July 20, 2015

Dr. Ackerman further notes that there are new guidelines regarding long QT syndrome athletes, published in 2013. They state that an athlete with long QT syndrome who wishes to remain a competitive athlete should see an expert, who will help determine whether to continue in sports. This is a clear departure from the previous international guidelines, which stated that a person with the long QT diagnosis was summarily disqualified from all competitive sports.

Delaney Middlebrook is a major reason for this change in guidelines.

Delaney's long QT diagnosis presents no obstacle to her playing for HV71. The Riksserien has no rules that prohibit players with her diagnosis from playing, so the question does not even arise, and the surgery she underwent in 2010 eliminated concerns regarding an "episode." In fact, shortly after Delaney arrives in Sweden her diagnosis becomes public knowledge when the October edition of *Let's Play Hockey* magazine comes out, with a front-page article about her extraordinary journey, headlined "It Takes Heart."

Chapter 57

Jönköping lies in the county of Småland, on the southern shore of Sweden's second largest lake, Lake Vättern. Stockholm is 180 miles to the northeast and Gothenburg 90 miles due east. Jönköping was founded in 1284, and by 2015 its metro area was home to almost 134,000 people. The city is passionate about ice hockey, and HV71 is their team. The club was formed by the merger of two already existing clubs, Husqvarna and Vätterstad, in 1971—hence the name HV71.

Both the men's and women's teams play in the Kinnarps Arena (today called Husqvarna Garden), with a capacity of 7,000 fans, including 1,100 standing. An NHL-size Daktronics scoreboard hangs over center ice, and the rink also features a sports bar, cafe and even a separate top-tier off-ice training facility. The HV71 men's games are always standing room only. The women's team, although not a big crowd draw or revenue producer like the men, is treated as a fully professional operation, right down to their own first-class dressing room.

Delaney will not be the only American wearing the blue, white and gold for the HV71 women's team in the 2015-16 Riksserien. Joining her as a teammate, roommate and defense partner is Emma Stauber, from Duluth, Minnesota, a former college captain at Minnesota–Duluth. She and Delaney have met before, at USA National Camp. They both arrive in Jönköping in early August, in time for a team training and bonding camp on the Swedish west coast: three days of workouts, swimming and fishing, and campfires on the beach at night. Delaney's new teammates include veteran Swedish Olympian Jenni Asserholt, who was an instructor at SwISH camp in 2009, and another Swedish Olympian, Fanny Rask, whose brother Victor skates in the NHL. In addition to the Swedes on the roster there are two Canadians, a Finn, a German and a Norwegian. The coach is 49-year-old Ulf Johansson, who has led the team since their first season in 2013-14.

At this time clubs in the Riksserien directly pay only some of their players, generally the top domestic stars and some foreigners. Delaney and Emma are both paid directly by HV71, enough so that they can live comfortably. They live in half a duplex provided by the club and take the bus everywhere they go, just as many Swedes do. In addition, both accept jobs as instructors at an international school, an opportunity provided by an HV71 supporter. Although they earn a separate paycheck for this work, they don't do it for the money; they do it to have something meaningful during the day. Delaney teaches English, math and science to high school students, learning on the job how to be a teacher. Her Sweden experience is indeed turning out to be much more than hockey.

The 2015-16 Riksserien, and Delaney's career as a pro, begins in early September with a home game against AIK. Cathy and I excitedly watch the livestream on the computer and see Delaney wearing the dark blue with gold trim uniform, HV71 on the front, number 7 and the name Middlebrook on the back. Delaney and Emma start on defense and are on the ice for over 40 percent of the game, including every time HV71 is shorthanded. In a close contest AIK prevails 2-1, but Delaney has played very well. We talk afterward, and her delight resonates to us through the phone from seven time zones away.

HV71 proves to be a solid team, although not one at the top of the Riksserien. Delaney thrives playing a regular shift and having the responsibility of being on the ice when the game is on the line. She is completely alive again, set free from three years of hockey oppression. HV71 and the Swedish Riksserien are everything for her that RPI was not.

HV71 has four home games in a six-day span in late October. It is a perfect week for me to visit and watch Delaney play in person. I fly to Amsterdam and then to Linköping, where friends Lars Wennerholm and his family live. Lars drives me the hour to Jönköping for the next night's game, HV71 vs AIK again. This time HV71 wins, 2-0, and it is another strong performance from Delaney. She and Emma are on the ice defending for the final two minutes after AIK has pulled their goalie.

HV71 wins the next two games also, setting up a Sunday showdown with league-leading Luleå.

They are led by Finnish star Michelle Karvinen, who played at the University of North Dakota for three years, scoring 131 points in only 87 NCAA games. Luleå is a fast-skating, highly skilled team that uses the entire surface of the big European ice. They prove too much for HV71, winning by a final score of 7-4.

Still, as I return home the next day, I haven't felt this good for Delaney since her freshman year at Niagara.

Chapter 58

In mid-November Cathy and I are in Chicago for a Saturday wedding. It turns into a very late night. Even so, I am awake at 6 the next morning to watch Delaney and HV71 skate against Sundsvall. I see Delaney score her first Riksserien goal, picking up a pass in the high slot and putting the puck under the crossbar, over the goalie's right shoulder. It's the game winner, and it shows up on YouTube as the Riksserien goal of the week.

Cathy and I travel to Sweden on the day before Thanksgiving 2015, flying in to Linköping and spending the night with the Wennerholms before driving to Jönköping the next day to watch HV71 play. Unfortunately for HV71 Emma Stauber has decided to go back to Minnesota the week before, and high-scoring Canadian forward Jenna Smith breaks her foot. Delaney will miss Emma, both as a roommate and defense partner, but also as one of the two Americans playing for HV71. They have been featured in the Swedish press, interviewed on television and been the subject of multiple online articles and tweets. Delaney, however, will not be the lone American for long. Kyla Sanders, a four-year forward for Wisconsin's D1 varsity, joins HV71, and she and Delaney become good friends.

While in Jönköping Cathy and I stay in a hotel directly across the street from the ice arena. We watch three home games and Cathy is thrilled to see Delaney skating as a pro and feeling complete hockey fulfillment for the first time in years. We also rent a car, and the three of us explore the countryside around Jönköping and Lake Vättern. The IKEA store in Jönköping has begun serving a traditional Swedish Christmas meal, buffet style. The three of us join hundreds of Jönköpingsbor (people from Jönköping), and I fill my plate multiple times.

Our week in Sweden ends in Stockholm, watching Delaney and HV71 face Djurgården the night before we are to fly home. Cathy and I have taken the train from Jönköping while Delaney has ridden the HV71 team bus. Before the game I see Nils Ekman. He tells me he is happy that Delaney is playing in Sweden for a good club and a good team.

The game ends 4-0 for Djurgården, clearly the better team. But Delaney has played a strong game, both defensively and in bringing the puck up ice on the attack. After the game I again see Nils, who tells me he was impressed with Delaney's play.

Two weeks later Delaney returns to Minneapolis for the week-long Christmas break. Spending the break with her in Minnesota is an HV71 teammate, Sandra Hedberg. They skate each morning in Drake Arena at St. Paul Academy, but in the afternoon they are at the Mall of America and other shopping meccas, and each evening Sandra experiences the nightlife of the Twin Cities, including New Year's Eve as she joins Delaney and her former classmates from SPA to celebrate. When the week ends, Sandra thanks Cathy and me and tells us she had a great experience. She says that being a hockey player can be about so much more than hockey. She is more than right.

Chapter 59

In late January 2016 I am in Moscow, riding on a bus from Sheremetyevo Airport to Domodedovo Airport for a flight to Ulyanovsk. I am watching Delaney and HV71 play a Riksserien game on my phone.

Or at least I am trying to. The connection fades in and out. The game is tied in the third period and I watch as Delaney crashes the net for a rebound. I see her shoot ... but then the connection is completely lost. I do not find out until many hours later, after I have arrived in Ulyanovsk, that the puck went in for the game winner.

HV71 finishes the Riksserien regular season in sixth place with 19 wins and 17 losses, having scored 90 goals and given up 109. Delaney scores two goals and seven assists, but most important she has played strong defense all year, ending the season at plus-3. She also finishes with the second highest number of penalty minutes in the Riksserien, a testament to her aggressive, physical play.

In the playoffs the top three teams get to choose their opponent for the quarterfinal round. First-place Luleå picks eighth-place MoDo. Second-place Linköping, the defending Swedish champion, picks sixth-place HV71. The explanation given is travel time and expense. HV71, in Jönköping, is an hour's trip from Linköping; seventh-place finisher Leksand is four-and-a-half hours distant.

Linköping is confident of victory regardless of their opponent. But when HV71 wins the first game in the best-of-three series by 3-0, the decision-makers for Linkoping must be wondering if they made a mistake. The potentially decisive second game is dead-even going into the third period, 2-2. The defending champions are on the ropes.

Linköping's first-line left winger is another Swedish Olympian, Pernilla Winberg, a 100-point scorer in her NCAA career at Minnesota-Duluth, and, as fate would have it, an instructor at SwISH Camp when Delaney attended in 2009. But now Delaney and Winberg have a different relationship: Delaney, all grown up and skating in HV71's first defensive pair, is Winberg's aggressive tormentor. But with 10 minutes left, Linköping scores the go-ahead goal in what ends as a 3-2 victory, even as Delaney's shot from the point hits the post with only minutes remaining. The next night Linköping takes the series in a emphatic 4-0 victory. They'll get to the championship series, but there they fall, two games to one, against Luleå.

Delaney's first Riksserien season has ended on a disappointing note. Nevertheless, it has been an extraordinarily positive experience, having proven herself a very good defender in one of the world's top women's leagues. She calls the season the best hockey experience of her life.

But hockey is not yet over for Delaney in the spring of 2016. Soon after HV71's elimination she is asked by top Swedish First Division club Göteborg to join them for a game against the Norwegian national team. Already skating for Göteborg is Delaney's teammate and roommate from her freshman year at Niagara, Kalli Funk. It is Delaney's first game against a national team, and although Göteborg loses the club offers Delaney a contract for the following season.

Several weeks later Delaney is again facing a national team, this time in a two-game set against China, while skating for Djurgården. Delaney has not yet signed a contract with HV71 for the following season, so when the Stockholm club extends its invitation, there are no conflicts. In Stockholm she stays at the apartment of one of the main promoters of Chinese hockey, Per-Erik Holmström, and has Easter dinner with Djurgården goalie Lovisa Berndtsson and her family.

Djurgården wins twice against China, with Delaney playing two strong games. The Djurgården coach, Jared Cipparone, talks to her about playing for the club the following season. She is very interested.

In early June, Delaney signs a contract and makes it official: she will play for Djurgården in the 2016-17 Swedish women's elite league, which has been renamed the Svenska Damhockeyligan—the SDHL.

In late June Delaney also signs her first NHL contract, though not as a player. HV71 men's player Jacob Moveare is a fourth-round draft pick of the L.A. Kings. When he comes to the U.S. to finalize his deal he meets Delaney in Chicago and asks her to sign the contract as the witness. Moveare will make his NHL debut with the Kings in January 2022.

XIV. Stockholm's Pride

Chapter 60

In between skating for Göteborg against Norway and Djurgården against China, I meet Delaney in Dublin for St. Patrick's Day. Along with her deep Irish roots, her very name, Delaney, is Gaelic in origin, meaning "child of dark defiance." It is time for her to come home to Ireland.

We connect at the Dublin airport and head into the city, where we stay in a hotel at the center of the festivities. We walk everywhere and see everything there is to see in Dublin. On our way to the Jameson Distillery we get lost, but it appears there is a higher reason for this. On a street we never would have walked we see "Delaney's Bar." Of course we go in, only to discover it is gentlemen-only day at Delaney's; no women allowed. I explain our Irish heritage and that the young lady, my daughter, is named Delaney. With that, the bar's patrons immediately agree to make an exception to the no-women rule, and within minutes Delaney is behind the bar, pouring pints of Guinness.

The next day we rent a car and drive to Crossmaglen in County Armagh, the town our Irish ancestors came from. "You are going to bandit country," I am told by the rental agent, "right on the border of Northern Ireland." The town square of Crossmaglen is called Sniper Alley, the rental agent says, because of the many British soldiers shot there by the Irish Republican Army. I respond that Delaney and I are simply going home.

In Crossmaglen Delaney and I stay at the hotel located at the west end of Sniper Alley. Our goal is to find the cemetery where our direct ancestor was buried over 400 years before. All we really know is that it lies in the middle of a cow pasture. At lunch at the hotel, a woman is celebrating her 90th birthday with a somewhat younger friend. A cake is presented to her, and Delaney and I join the others in the restaurant in singing "Happy Birthday." When I extend to her my personal birthday wishes she thanks me, and notes that I am American. I describe for her the cemetery Delaney and I are looking for. She knows it. So does a young lady at a nearby table. She draws out specific directions for us to find it. "The road will end at a cow pasture," she tells us. "You must then walk a ways to the cemetery. Watch out for the bull, though. He doesn't like strangers."

Delaney and I find the cemetery and the grave of our ancestor. She places her hand on the gravestone and looks defiantly in the direction of Northern Ireland, while I take a photo. She is a true Irish child of dark defiance.

In April Delaney flies to Rome to spend five days with family friends, the Ragone family. Vittorio Ragone shows Delaney as much of Rome as can be seen in such a short time; he even takes her to the beach on the Tyrrhenian Sea. In the span of only weeks Delaney has gone from ice rinks in Sweden skating against Norway and China, to an Irish graveyard in the middle of a cow pasture, to the ancient Colosseum in Rome where gladiators fought and died. After future seasons in Sweden she will visit most of Europe, ski the Alps, sunbathe on the coast of Spain, dance at a music festival in Amsterdam, and spend Midsommar in the north of Sweden. Truly, the opportunities that come from being a hockey player can wind up being so much more than hockey.

Chapter 61

The city of Stockholm stands amid an archipelago in Mälaren, a large lake whose outlets eventually flow into the Baltic Sea. Although people have lived at Stockholm's location for some 8,000 years, the city itself was founded in 1252. Roughly 2.4 million people reside in the city and surrounding area, but Stockholm never seems crowded. It is without question one of the most beautiful cities in the world.

The Djurgården Sports Club—DIF—was founded in Stockholm in 1891. Djurgården is the name of the former hunting park owned by the Swedish royal family, and it is now the largest city park in Stockholm. Not surprisingly, the Djurgården sports team, clad in red, yellow and blue, are the favorites of Swedish royalty, including the current king, Carl Gustav XVI.

DIF—known as *Stockholms Stolthet*, or Stockholm's Pride—began playing ice hockey in 1922, and have gone on to win the Swedish men's ice hockey championship 16 times. It was only in the 2014-15 season that Djurgården adds women's ice hockey to its sports lineup. The Djurgården Dam (literally, ladies) skate in the same arena as the men, Hovet, which seats 8,000 spectators. They played their inaugural season in the Swedish East First Division, a step below the SDHL, and won every league game and every playoff game—going a perfect 30-0 with a goal difference of plus-254 (275 for, 21 against)—to advance to the SDHL.

In 2015-16, Djurgården Dam's first season in Sweden's top league, their first victory comes against HV71 and Delaney Middlebrook. DIF finished that season in fourth place and lost to Linköping in the playoff semifinals. The club has much higher aspirations for the 2016-17 campaign.

Delaney, who will wear number 77 on her Djurgården jersey, arrives in Stockholm in early August 2016 and moves into an apartment supplied by the club within walking distance of Hovet. Her roommate is Tori Hickel, a defender from Alaska who played college hockey for Northeastern and is new to Sweden. DIF kicks off the preseason with a team bonding and training weekend on an island in the Stockholm archipelago, as Delaney and Tori join their new teammates, who include Norwegians, a Dane, a Finn and a Russian. All have played for their national teams in world championships. Two skated for North Dakota, scoring over 100 career NCAA points each. The Swedish players include Olympic veteran Tina Enström, as well as several other past and future national team players. Delaney has even met three of her Djurgården teammates before, at the SwISH Hockey Camp in 2009. And Delaney is again playing with teammates whose brothers have skated in the NHL. The list is now five: Bortuzzo, Rask, Aho, Enström and Holøs.

DIF GM Nils Ekman talks about the addition of Delaney to the roster in newspapers and online. He says she has been added to the club for her strong, steady defensive play and for her experience at playing at a high level of competition. She is only 23, but he says she will be a good example for the younger blueliners, two still in their teens, to learn from.

In addition to hockey, Delaney is offered an internship by Anders Tollsten, CEO of the Swedish company Coromatic, which specializes in technically advanced and secure storage of computer systems, software and data. Anders has a daughter who plays hockey for Västerås, and he has followed Delaney's hockey career since she began skating for HV71. He hires Delaney to work in Coromatic's marketing department, her work hours structured so they don't conflict with her training or games. She takes the subway to and from work, pleased and proud to be both a pro hockey player and a corporate employee in Stockholm.

Chapter 62

In only the third year of its women's team's existence, Djurgarden has put together a powerful squad—yet it is not the class of the SDHL in 2016-17. That distinction belongs to defending SDHL champion Luleå, who will finish the regular season with a dominating 32-4 record.

Luleå is in the far north of Sweden, 451 miles from Stockholm, and although most SDHL travel to away games is done by bus, many teams fly to Luleå because the drive is too long. Hockey is *the* sport in Luleå, both men's and women's. The arena holds the SDHL attendance record, a sellout crowd of 6,220, for a regular-season game vs AIK in 2018. Luleå's roster is led by a core of the best players from Finland, including several who were high-level D1 college players in the U.S.

Cathy and I plan a visit to Stockholm in mid-October to see Delaney play three home games, including one against Luleå. But before we depart comes an announcement from the newly formed Minneapolis Hockey Hall of Fame.

The Hall's selection committee has chosen to induct Delaney Middlebrook as part of its inaugural class!

Delaney's fellow inductees include NHL legends and Stanley Cup winners, Olympic gold medalists, U.S National Team players, prominent coaches and builders of Minneapolis and USA hockey—people like Reed Larson, Mike Ramsey, Cully Dahlstrom, Badger Bob Johnson and Walter Bush Jr. The list of hockey legends and greats Delaney is to join goes back a hundred years. She is one of three women who will be enshrined at the induction ceremony, which is set for March 2017.

The committee informs me that Delaney's selection is based on two main factors. First, she is one of the most accomplished female hockey players to come out of Minneapolis; indeed she is only the second woman from the city to become a pro. And second, all she has accomplished has occurred while overcoming the tremendous obstacles presented by her heart condition and treatment, something the selection committee learned about from *Let's Play Hockey*'s 2015 article. Delaney's induction into the Minneapolis Hockey Hall of Fame as a charter member, they tell me, is a no-brainer.

Delaney is stunned and thrilled when we tell her about her Hall of Fame honor. But very quickly she sets her joy to the side—she is not done achieving and succeeding just yet. She is still driven to prove herself.

In Stockholm Cathy and I watch Delaney skate for Djurgården twice, and are on hand for a third game, vs. undefeated Luleå, at Hovet the afternoon before we are to fly home. We know that she hasn't been on the ice for a single goal-against during the season, an incredible stat tweeted and retweeted by a number of SDHL followers. She is clearly performing up to and beyond DIF's expectations.

So it goes against Luleå — Djurgården hands them their first defeat, 4–2. But neither Delaney nor her defense partner, Tori Hickel, are on the ice at the end of the game. Midway through the second period Hickel slides awkwardly into the boards and injures her knee. One shift later Delaney is battling a Luleå forward in front of the DIF net. Both players go down, but only one can get up; the Luleå player has fallen on Delaney's bent foot, which breaks a bone where the foot attaches to the ankle. It's the first significant injury that Delaney has sustained in her entire hockey career, going back to age 4. She is carried off the ice. Nils Ekman drives her to the hospital, with Cathy and me in the car as well.

Delaney is put in a cast and given crutches. She is told her injury will likely end her season. Perhaps ... but then again, when the doctor says that to Delaney, he has no idea whom he is talking to.

Afterward, Nils drives us all to Delaney's apartment. We agree that Cathy will still fly back to Minneapolis the next day, but I'll remain in Stockholm for several days to help Delaney while she decides whether to stay or go home.

Delaney decides that her season is not done. She stays off her foot completely for a week and learns how to maneuver on her crutches.

Then she starts attending Djurgården training sessions, all of them, staying in the gym to lift weights and pedal the exercise bike while the team practices on the ice. She also keeps working for Coromatic, getting to and from the office, on her crutches, via subway.

Six weeks later Delaney skates for the first time since the injury. She comes home for Christmas and skates almost every day at Drake Arena. And when she returns to Sweden after New Year's she makes her comeback against Linköping, in a game Djurgården wins. Sure enough, she is not on the ice for a single Linköping goal.

Chapter 63

Djurgården doesn't know if either Delaney or Tori Hickel will play again in 2016-17. Several weeks after the October game in which both are injured, DIF gets crushed in both ends of a two-game set at Luleå, 11-0 and 6-0. Clearly the defense needs bolstering, so the club signs two additional Americans, former Wisconsin Badger and U.S. Olympian Molly Engstrom and Sam Hansen, a former North Dakota defender and ex-teammate of Delaney on the Blades. Djurgården now has four American blueliners. In the entire SDHL, Sundsvall is the only other team with an American on the roster.

By mid-January, both Delaney and Tori are back, and Djurgården, loaded with eight healthy defenders, begins a winning streak that culminates with a 5-1 victory over Sundsvall in "The Outdoor Classic", the SDHL's first-ever outdoor game. Though DIF cannot catch Luleå, they do claim second place with a record of 26-10 for 79 points, one better than Linköping, whom they overtake on the final day of the season.

Goal scoring is not Djurgården's forte, with 97 goals scored to Luleå's 168 and Linköping's 138. But their defense is superb, as the team gives up only 73 goals—a figure that would be even more impressive were it not for the 17 given up that one disastrous weekend at Luleå. Delaney has done the job DIF asked her to do, and so much more, having come back from what was thought to be a season-ending injury. She ends the regular season a plus-11, on the ice for only two opponent goals at even strength.

In the best-of-three opening round of the SDHL playoffs, Djurgården faces seventh-place Leksand, struggling in the first game before prevailing, 2-1 in a shootout. In Game 2 they cruise to an 8-0 victory, led by Tina Enstrom's one goal and six assists.

Next up, Linköping in the semifinals. DIF wins the first game on the road, 3-0, but loses the second game at home, 3-1. That sets up the decisive game, again at Djurgården, to determine who will advance to the SDHL championship series. And it is DIF, as Delaney's host the previous Easter, goalie Lovisa Berndtsson, is brilliant, stopping 23 of 24 shots in a 4–1 triumph. Djurgården is through to the Swedish final.

The other semifinal pits defending champion Luleå vs fourth-place HV71, who finished the season almost 50 points behind Luleå. It should be no contest—but incredibly, Game 1 goes to a shootout that HV71 wins, 4-3. Even more incredible, the same thing happens in Game 2—another shootout, and another improbable 4-3 HV71 victory. Somehow the team from Jönköping has eliminated mighty Luleå. The SDHL's best-of-three final will take place between Djurgården and HV71, Delaney's former team.

Djurgarden won all four regular-season games vs. HV71 that year, and the previous year as well. In fact, DIF has never lost to HV71. That makes Djurgården the favorites, but after upsetting Luleå, HV71 looks like they might be a team of destiny.

Delaney is now paired with Norwegian Silje Holøs on defense. The other two defense pairs are Tori Hickel and Felicia Linder, and Molly Engstrom and Solveig Neunzert, with Swede Ida Press as the seventh back. Sam Hansen has a concussion and does not dress.

While three of Djurgården's defenders are American, HV71 has none on their entire roster—but they do dress eight non-Swedes, including three Canadians who all played D1 college hockey, and three Finns, a German and an Austrian, all of whom are national team players. This series will not be easy.

DIF wins a tense Game One at Jönköping, 1-0, as Delaney helps kill off four HV71 power plays. Game Two is set for Stockholm on March 18, 2017—the same day as the induction ceremonies for the Minneapolis Hockey Hall of Fame. Cathy, Ian and I watch on the computer as Djurgården falls behind, 2-1, but ties it up with a short-handed goal near the end of the first period. It's still tied, 3-3, after the second.

The game goes to the third period, the clock ticking down. Then, with less than nine minutes left, it happens: Hanna Olsson scores to make it 4-3 for DIF.

Now Djurgården must hang on. Delaney helps kill off a penalty with five minutes left. The score holds. With 90 seconds remaining HV71 pulls the goalie for an extra attacker, and with 19 seconds left,

DIF takes another penalty, for shooting the puck over the glass during a clearing attempt. HV71 now has a six-on-four skating advantage — but they cannot score! Djurgården wins the Swedish championship!

A wild celebration ensues on the ice as Delaney and her teammates don the traditional Swedish championship gold helmets, place their gold medals around their necks and hold the championship trophy triumphantly aloft.

Less than thirty minutes later, some 4,300 miles and seven time zones from Stockholm, Cathy, Ian and I accept Delaney Middlebrook's plaque and special jersey on her behalf as she is formally inducted into the Minneapolis Hockey Hall of Fame.

XV. A Perfect Ending

Chapter 64

The story of Delaney Middlebrook's hockey odyssey could beautifully, perfectly conclude on that March 2017 afternoon when she is inducted into the Minneapolis Hockey Hall of Fame at almost the same moment she became a Swedish champion. That'd be an ending befitting a film script, one in which the hero triumphs over all adversity.

But this is real life, and Delaney's story doesn't end just yet. There is one final leg in her hockey journey.

When we were in Dublin in 2016, Delaney said that at some point she wanted to go to graduate school and earn a master's degree, but that it wouldn't be possible while playing in the SDHL because the combined time commitments for hockey and school would be overwhelming. In Dublin she visited Trinity College and met with the admissions adviser. There was no guarantee, she was told, but her credentials made acceptance to Trinity likely.

In April 2017 Delaney made a new plan: attend graduate school in Sweden and, if possible, continue to play hockey in the First Division, a step down from the SDHL. The time commitment would be far less than playing in the SDHL, only 16 games compared to the SDHL's 36, along with much less travel time, plus training only three days a week, not five. She contacted several Swedish clubs, including Färjestad, located in Karlstad, on the northern end of Lake Vänern, the largest lake in the country. The city is home to Karlstad University, which offers two-year master's programs in business administration and economics.

Färjestad signs Delaney in July, and in August she leaves Minneapolis for Karlstad, where she'll work toward her master's degree while skating in the Swedish Western First Division.

Färjestad BK was formed as a bandy club in 1932 (the BK stands for "Bollklubb"), but it did not play ice hockey until 1956. Since then, however, FBK has won nine Swedish men's hockey championships. The Färjestad women's team began play in 2014, in the same 9,000-seat arena as the men, Löfbergs Arena. They have competed in the First Division all three of their seasons, winning the league each year with near perfect records, but falling short in the promotion playoffs every time. They have never advanced to the SDHL.

Rather than sharing an apartment with a teammate her first year in Karlstad, Delaney lives with the Öhman family, Matti and Pia, who welcome her into their house. The Öhmans are big supporters of Färjestad hockey; both Matti and his son are former players. Delaney decides she will wear number 27 on her green and gold FBK jersey, the same number Matti and Pia's son wore. She also forms a special bond with Matti and Pia's granddaughter Molly. Delaney is now truly a member of a Swedish family.

The Öhmans don't have to drive Delaney anywhere—the club has supplied her with a car, complete with the Färjestad logo, Delaney's name and number, all painted in green and gold on the side.

Färjestad's club motto is emblazoned on signs around Löfbergs Arena and on its green-and-gold souvenir T-shirts: *Stort hjärta— Hårt arbete*: "Big heart—Hard work." The word *stort*, however, has a much richer meaning to Färjestad's players and supporters than simply "big." It signifies the courageous, bold, stout hearts of FBK. The motto fits Delaney perfectly.

The goal of the Färjestad women's team for 2017-18 is to win their league again, but this time to win in the promotion playoffs and advance to the SDHL. In addition to Delaney, they have brought in Canadian Jenna Smith, who played for HV71 in 2015-16 before breaking her ankle. The roster also includes two Norwegians, with the rest of the players native Swedes, only one of whom has played in the SDHL. The coach is a Swede and a former NHL draft choice.

In late August 2017, I am in Karlstad, watching Delaney and FBK lose 3-1 to the Norwegian national team. But I didn't come to Sweden to see Delaney. Instead, I am there as an assistant coach with the Minnesota Whitecaps of the National Women's Hockey League, who are playing four games in Stockholm against SDHL teams—two vs. Djurgården, one against AIK and one against SDE. The Whitecaps were missing their five Olympians, but still, the entire roster consists of former D1 college players. They are a strong team, yet they lose all four games to their SDHL hosts. (The following September, 2018 SDHL champions Luleå will defeat NWHL champions Metropolitan Riveters, 4-2, in the first women's Champions Cup, bolstering the SDHL's status as a truly elite women's hockey league.)

I am in Karlstad for only 24 hours. As I board the train for Stockholm the next morning, I help an 18-year-old load his hockey gear. His name is Joel Eriksson Ek, and he is headed to Minnesota for the NHL Wild's training camp.

Now it is March and I have returned with Cathy to watch Färjestad in the qualifying playoffs for the SDHL. They have run away with their league once again, with a 16-0 record, outscoring their opponents by 141-6. Jenna Smith leads the league in scoring, averaging 4 points per game. Delaney is the league's top defense scorer with 5 goals and 12 assists; she is also second in the league in penalties. In the best-of-three first round, FBK sweeps Troja/Ljungby, edging them, 2-1, in Game 1, and beating them, 5-0, while piling up a 50-20 shot advantage in Game 2.

After the second game, Delaney, Cathy and I join Jenna Smith and Jenna's host family, Ulf and Pia Sterner, at their home for a pizza and beer party. On January 27, 1965, Ulf Sterner became the first European to play in the NHL. He has amazing stories to share about his hockey experiences, and we want to hear them all.

Next up is the final promotion/relegation series, vs. Göteborg, the last-place finisher in the SDHL. The first game of the best-of-three series takes place in Karlstad, where Göteborg shuts down the FBK offense, winning 4-1. The series then moves to Gothenburg, where it is win or go back to the First Division for Färjestad. Will FBK do a repeat of their previous three years, compiling dominant regular seasons, only to falter at the final hurdle?

The first period ends even at 1-1, but Göteborg takes command in the second with two unanswered goals. In the third, Goteborg's tight defense stymies FBK, killing off the game and with it Färjestad's SDHL dream for another year. The 3-1 score emphasizes the gap that exists between Sweden's First Division and the SDHL.

The next day Cathy and I fly home. Delaney, however, enters the hospital in Karlstad for emergency surgery on a ruptured cyst. For the previous week the rupture made it impossible for her to sit comfortably or to sleep, yet somehow she still managed to play against Troja/Ljungby and Goteborg. She remains in the hospital for three days.

In late June Delaney returns to Minneapolis. She needs one more year at Karlstad University, including writing her thesis, to get her master's. She must decide: play a second season of hockey for Färjestad, or hang up her skates to concentrate on her degree.

Chapter 65

Delaney returns to Sweden and Karlstad in mid-August 2018 for the final year of her master's program. Her thesis addresses sustainability and renewal of resources within Swedish companies, and the following May it will be accepted and awarded with High Distinction.

But when she arrives in Karlstad, Delaney still hasn't decided whether she will play hockey again for FBK, Contract negotiations ensue, and when she signs her new deal it includes a clause that allows her to transfer to an SDHL team at any time during the season, with no limitation or restriction. It's an adroit move: she knows that by mid-January her in-class work at Karlstad University will be completed and she can work on her thesis remotely—thus enabling her to return to the SDHL and finish her hockey career at the highest level. Clearly she learned some things from her summer studying negotiations at the London School of Economics.

In the third week of January 2019, it is time for Delaney to move. She leaves Färjestad and the First Division, signing a contract to finish the season with Göteborg in the SDHL—the same team that defeated FBK in the previous year's promotion playoffs. With Göteborg she will finish her career in a black and gold uniform, wearing No. 5—the same number she wore in youth hockey and in her six years of high school hockey. Gothenburg is only a two-hour train ride from Karlstad. So she'll stay with teammates when she is in Gothenburg for training and home games, and meeting the team bus for away games.

Delaney leaves behind a Färjestad side that once again leads the Western First Division with an undefeated record, and she is again the league-leading defense scorer. She also leaves behind her Japanese defense partner, Nachi Fujimoto, and her two best friends on the team, both from Holland. In Färjestad's second game after Delaney leaves, the club loses its first league match in two years.

Delaney joins a Göteborg team that once again lies at the bottom of the SDHL standings. Only six league games remain on the schedule, and she will play in all six—but Göteborg has really brought Delaney in for the crucial qualifying playoffs against the First Division champions. It is entirely possible that Göteborg and Delaney will face Färjestad in the promotion/relegation final.

One of Göteborg's final games of the regular season is a 6-2 loss at Leksand. Afterward, the players and coaches board the bus for the six-hour ride back to Gothenburg. Most are asleep when at 1 a.m. the bus leaves the road in a heavy snowstorm, turns partway onto its right side and slides into a ditch at high speed. It comes to a stop just before striking a large tree.

As the bus tipped, the players were thrown to the right. That made the bus start tipping over even more to the right, so one of the coaches yelled for the players to scramble back to the left to keep the bus from going over completely, and to put their seat belts on in case it did. The door, wedged into a large snowdrift, would not open. They were stuck, so there they waited, many of the players screaming and crying, until a rescue squad arrived to get them out. During the wait Delaney called me from her cellphone, whispering to me what had happened, as if the bus would completely tip over if she spoke too loudly. The rescue squad put supports under the bus and dug away the snow blocking the door. But the door was still jammed, so they cut an opening to allow the players and coaches to exit. One at a time they left their seats and crawled through the opening, until all were out. They then made their way through waist-deep snow up to the road, where they were loaded onto another bus two hours after the accident.

Amazingly, none of the players sustained serious injuries. All would play in the SDHL qualifying series the following week.

Göteborg meets SDHL aspirant Karlskrona HK in March to determine which team will play in the SDHL in 2019-20. Karlskrona has won the South First Division, and crushed their opponent, the East champion, in the playoffs. (Färjestad crashed out in the opening round.) Karlskrona is led by several Canadians, including a seven-goal scorer in the opening series. But Karlskrona will learn the same lesson Färjestad learned the previous year against Göteborg—there's a big difference between the speed and tempo of the SDHL and the First Division.

Göteborg wins Game 1, 2-0. Delaney and her defense mates are in the seven-goal skater's face the entire game. Game 2 takes place in Karlskrona on a Saturday afternoon. Cathy and I watch on our computer, even though game time for us is 6 a.m.

Göteborg takes a 1-0 lead in the first period. In the second period we watch as they score again, off a two-on-one break with the pass going to a Göteborg skater who fakes right, then brings the puck across and slides it into the left side of the net. Was that Delaney who just scored? Yes, it was!

Late in the second period Karlskrona tallies on a power play, cutting the deficit to 2-1. They try to equalize but Göteborg holds them off. Then, late in the third period, Göteborg seals the victory with a third goal. It is done: Göteborg will stay in the SDHL.

In her final game—the last step in a journey that began almost 21 years earlier with a little girl telling her father that if he lets her play hockey she will never quit—Delaney Middlebrook has scored the game winner, the goal that will keep her team in Sweden's top league. She has completed her improbable run and achieved far more than she had dreamed of when, at 13, she announced that she wanted to be an all-state and D1 player. Cathy, Ian and I are so proud of her, so proud of all she has accomplished and overcome. I feel that somewhere, somehow, Delaney's grandparents, John and Phyllis, know, and they are happy. And I realize that for the first time in so very many years I am no longer looking into the abyss. I can live in peace.

I am then overcome by a powerful emotion, a certainty, that someone else has been following Delaney throughout her life and her hockey journey, her refusal to succumb to long QT syndrome, the beta blockers and the tremendous challenges she faced. It is Delaney's sister, Annalise, who wanted to live and fought so hard to do so. Delaney has lived and achieved, something that was denied to Annalise—but she is proud of her younger sister and I believe the most pleased of any of us. I realize that on the day she died in my arms, the light that was her did not go out forever. I simply couldn't see it anymore. But now I can. And I also know that now, she can rest in peace.

And that is the end of this story.

With Immense Gratitude

Behind every story of triumph over adversity is a support system of people. This is especially true for Delaney Middlebrook. These are four people essential to who she became as a hockey player and as a person:

Dr. Michael Ackerman, Delaney's heart specialist, who cared for her as if she were his own daughter, supporting her efforts to continue to compete, even as the rules said she couldn't.

Winny Brodt, the women's hockey icon, who trained Delaney to be a high-level player while opening the doors of opportunity for her — the best friend a hockey-playing girl could ever have

Kevin McMullen, the Minneapolis girls hockey coach and Delaney's longtime mentor and friend, who helped her believe she was good enough to achieve her dreams.

Bryn Roberts, St. Paul Academy Head of School, who, from the first time he saw 13-year-old Delaney play in high school, was her advocate and had her back as a hockey player, a student and a person.

About the Author

Chris Middlebrook is the father of the girl who played hockey. He was born, raised and still resides in south Minneapolis. He earned a Bachelor of Science in Russian from Gustavus Adolphus College in 1979 and his Juris Doctor from the University of Minnesota Law School in 1983. In 1984 he married the love of his life, law school classmate Cathy Young. Before beginning his law career Chris spent two years playing the sport of bandy in Sweden, the first North American to do so, and has continued his bandy career as a player, coach and president of the American Bandy Association. A member of the USA Bandy Hall of Fame, he has represented the United States internationally as a player and as coach of both the men's and women's national teams. In 1995 Chris founded the law firm Middlebrook Law. Beginning in 1999 he was recognized every year until his retirement in 2017 as both a Super Lawyer and as one of the Best Lawyers in Minnesota. In 2019 he published his first book, *The Bandy Chronicles: My Pursuit of a Forgotten Sport*, which has since been translated into Russian, Swedish and Italian.